Research Foundation Literature Review

PERFORMANCE ATTRIBUTION

History and Progress

Carl Bacon, CIPM

CFA Institute
Research
Foundation

Statement of Purpose

The CFA Institute Research Foundation is a not-for-profit organization established to promote the development and dissemination of relevant research for investment practitioners worldwide.

Cover photo credit: egon69 / E+ / Getty Images

ISBN 978-1-944960-89-6

Contents

Introduction 1
Early Development 3
Foundations 10
Multiperiod Analysis 15
Multicurrency Attribution 20
Types of Attribution 23
Risk-Adjusted Attribution 26
Fixed-Income Attribution 27
Other Attribution Issues 30
Conclusion: The Evolution of Attribution Methodologies 33
Bibliography 35

CE Qualified Activity CFA Institute

This publication qualifies for 2.5 CE credits under the guidelines of the CFA Institute Continuing Education Program.

Performance Attribution

History and Progress

Carl Bacon, CIPM
Chief Adviser, StatPro

Introduction

The objective of performance attribution, as stated by Menchero (2000), is to explain portfolio performance relative to a benchmark, identify the sources of excess return, and relate them to active decisions by the portfolio manager. Hensel, Ezra, and Ilkiw (1991) defined attribution as the "mathematical process of explaining an investment return by relating it to the different risk-taking decisions implicit in the portfolio, and the extent to which each of those risks was rewarded or penalized in the capital markets" (p. 66). Colin (2014) said that the purpose of attribution is to disentangle the fund's overall return into the component returns generated by each risk.

In other words, attribution measures which of your investment decisions about the portfolio's underlying risks worked and which did not. This information is critical business intelligence for anyone involved in selecting, managing, or marketing investments. As the authors noted above, Fischer and Wermers (2013) considered attribution analysis to be the "description and the quantification of key factors on the returns of investment portfolios" (p. 395). DiBartolomeo (2003) considered performance attribution to be the process of disentangling component portions of the observed returns to draw conclusions about the strengths and weaknesses of the investment process.

Note that these definitions are similar. The central question of an attribution analysis is thus the following: To which investment decisions can the active return of a portfolio relative to its benchmark be traced over a given period?

Formally, Bacon (2008) stated that "performance attribution is a technique used to quantify the excess return of a portfolio against its benchmark into the active decisions of the investment decision process" (p. 117). Murira and Sierra (2006) considered performance attribution the *ex post* complement to the *ex ante* risk decomposition provided by the risk measurement process.

"Performance attribution" is, therefore, perhaps a misleading term: As these descriptions suggest, the *excess*, *active*, or *relative* return is examined, not the whole of the return (or absolute return). "Relative return attribution" or simply "attribution analysis" is perhaps better terminology. Absolute attribution, or simply contribution analysis, would explain the sources of return of a portfolio in isolation rather than in comparison with a benchmark.

As described in Bacon (2008), attribution analysis is a critical management tool for several key stakeholders in the asset management process. Above all, it is the main tool for performance analysts because it allows them to ensure that the return is correct. It allows them to participate in the investment decision process by enabling them to demonstrably add value and thus justify their salary and effort. Return attribution, together with risk analysis, is the tool that allows the analyst to understand the sources of return in the portfolio and to communicate that understanding to portfolio managers, senior managers, and asset owners.

Investment management firms themselves, and the portfolio managers they employ, are also major users of attribution analysis. Attribution analysis provides a good starting point for a dialogue with asset owners on the positive and negative aspects of recent performance. Attribution analysis can be used aggressively to identify underperformance early and provide clients with a thorough explanation of underperformance and, hopefully, a rationale for improving performance. Attribution analysis is also crucial in gaining the confidence of asset owners by demonstrating a good understanding of the drivers of performance.

Portfolio managers inhabit the front office of asset management firms; typically, performance analysts inhabit the middle office. The back office is also able to use daily, security-level attribution, however, as a diagnostic tool for identifying pricing and transaction errors.

Bacon (2008) also stated that "senior management take an active interest in attribution analysis to provide them with a tool to monitor their portfolio managers. They will be keen to identify performance outliers—good or bad—and to ensure that value is added consistently across the firm" (p. 117).

Hence, attribution analysis has numerous uses across a wide range of asset management stakeholders.

Lord (1997) suggested that the characteristics of a good attribution system would include the following:

- a consistent approach for analysing returns,
- a solid theoretical framework for valuation,
- the ability to analyse portfolios and indexes consistently,
- attribution factors consistent with decision variables of the portfolio strategy process,

- summary attribution analysis constructed from security details, which themselves should be available for inspection,
- transactions, and
- robust analytic systems and high-quality data to provide meaningful attribution results.

Murira and Sierra (2006) suggested that there is general agreement that an attribution framework must meet two key requirements:

1. It should be consistent with the investment decision-making process of the portfolio. Performance attribution is most useful if it mirrors the investment management process because, in that case, it enables the identification and explanation of the sources of excess return.
2. It should be compatible with the organization's performance measurement and risk measurement systems. Managers would have difficulty making effective use of the information provided by the performance attribution process if the data being explained by this process were inconsistent with the data originating from the internal risk and performance systems.

As in many literature reviews, here the approach to the task is historical—beginning with the first attempts at performance measurement, about a half-century ago, and progressing to the present.

Early Development

Arguably, comparative performance measurement began with Dietz's (1966) *Pension Funds: Measuring Investment Performance* and the Bank Administration Institute (BAI 1968) report *Measuring the Investment Performance of Pension Funds for the Purpose of Inter-Fund Comparison*. The purpose of the BAI study was to develop methods of comparing the performance of pension funds to differentiate between the abilities of their respective managers. The main conclusions of their study are still relevant:

1. Performance measurement returns should be based on market value, not cost.
2. Returns should be total returns.
3. Returns should be time weighted.
4. Performance should include risk as well as return.
5. Funds should be classified according to their investment objectives.

Although the report did not recommend the use of attribution analysis—instead, emphasizing the importance of the total return of the portfolio—it did suggest that comparison of various sector returns within the portfolio might be useful. Interestingly, Eugene Fama was later invited to write and wrote the chapter on risk for this report.

Fama Decomposition. Fama was the first to fully delve into the subject of attribution analysis, which he did in "Components of Investment Performance" (Fama 1972). In this seminal paper, Fama suggested breaking down observed return into the part resulting from ability to pick the best securities at a given level of risk (which he at the time called "selectivity"; now, it is often referred to as "selection return") and the part that is the result of predictions of general market price movements—that is, the return from systematic risk—as follows:

$$\underbrace{\bar{r}-\bar{r}_F}_{\text{Excess return}}=\underbrace{\bar{r}-\beta\times(\bar{b}-r_F)-\bar{r}_F}_{\text{Selectivity}}+\underbrace{\beta\times(\bar{b}-r_F)}_{\text{Systematic risk}}, \tag{1}$$

where:

$\bar{r}$ = average portfolio return
$\bar{b}$ = average market or benchmark return
β = portfolio systematic risk
$\bar{r}_F$ = average risk-free rate

If a portfolio is fully diversified, it incurs no specific risk and the total portfolio risk will equal the systematic risk. Portfolio managers will give up diversification, however, to seek additional return. Therefore, the return from selectivity can be broken down into (1) the additional return required to justify sacrificing a given amount of diversification and (2) the net return from selectivity (the remainder of the manager's value added). The return from selectivity is equivalent to Jensen's alpha, α.

The term "diversification" (used in a different context from the one we would understand today) "is the return required to justify moving away from the benchmark and taking on specific risk" (Bacon 2013, p. 88). To calculate this diversification return, you first have to calculate the effective beta required such that systematic risk alone is equivalent to the total portfolio risk. This beta is the Fama beta, calculated as follows:

$$\beta_F=\frac{\sigma}{\sigma_b}, \tag{2}$$

where:

σ = portfolio risk
σ_b = benchmark risk

Therefore, the return required to justify not being fully diversified is calculated by using the difference between the Fama beta and the portfolio beta as follows:

$$d = (\beta_F - \beta) \times (\bar{b} - \bar{r}_F). \tag{3}$$

Note that the "Fama beta will always be greater than or equal to the portfolio beta since total risk is greater than or equal to the systematic risk of the portfolio" (Bacon 2013, p. 89).

The net return from selectivity ("net selectivity," for short) is the remaining return from selectivity after deducting the amount of return required to justify not being fully diversified:

Net selectivity = Selectivity – Diversification.

$$\text{Net selectivity} = S_{\text{Net}} = \alpha - d.$$

If net selectivity is negative, the portfolio manager has failed to justify the loss of diversification.

Timing is the return from the manager's variations in systematic risk (beta) around some policy or target amount:

$$\underbrace{\beta \times (\bar{b} - \bar{r}_F)}_{\substack{\text{Systematic} \\ \text{Risk}}} = \underbrace{(\beta - \beta_I) \times (\bar{b} - \bar{r}_F)}_{\substack{\text{Manager's Systematic} \\ \text{Risk or Timing}}} + \underbrace{\beta_I \times (\bar{b} - \bar{r}_F)}_{\substack{\text{Investor's Systematic} \\ \text{Risk}}}, \tag{4}$$

where β_I = the investor's systematic risk or target risk.

Figure 1 illustrates Fama's decomposition for portfolio *A*. A' represents the return from systematic risk (conventional beta) plus the risk-free rate, and A'' represents the return from the Fama beta plus the risk-free rate.

Fama's (1972) "Components of Investment Performance" is the first paper to seriously analyse the sources of return of an investment portfolio and, therefore, represents the birth of attribution analysis.

Notional Funds. In response to the BAI (1968) paper, a working group was set up towards the end of 1970 by the Society of Investment Analysts (SIA) in the United Kingdom to make recommendations on the subject

Figure 1. Fama Decomposition

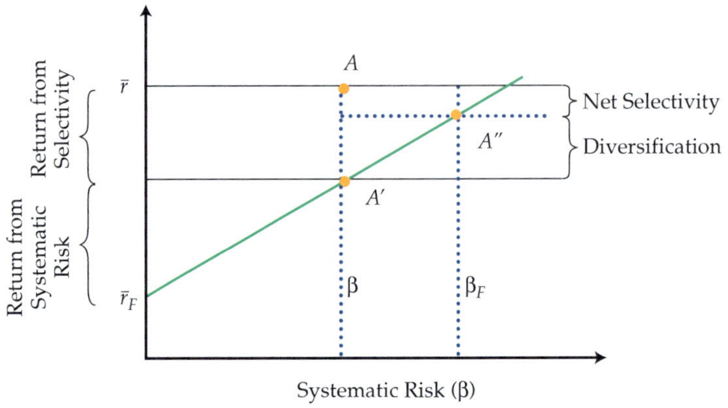

Source: Redrawn from a diagram in Fama (1972).

of portfolio performance measurement for pension funds. Its approach, eventually published in 1972 (SIA 1972), had two aims: (1) the determination of a standard method of calculating a portfolio's return, so that funds could be fairly compared, and (2) the decomposition of the performance of the fund into two components—selection of individual stocks and selection of stock sectors. The first aim is achieved by calculating the time-weighted rate of return using a simple approximation (which later became known as the analyst's test method and ultimately became redundant as more accurate time-weighted returns became available). The second aim, the analysis of performance, is produced by constructing "notional funds" based on market indexes and comparing them with actual funds.

This early work dealt with equity-market sectors as the macro level of selection and securities within the sectors as the micro level, but common practice now is to regard asset *classes* (stocks, bonds, etc.) as the macro level and securities within the asset class as the micro level. Thus, our discussion will proceed from this latter starting point.

The working group established two notional funds as follows:

- a fully restrained fund (index returns, benchmark weights) and
- a partly restrained fund (index returns, actual weights).

Note that the actual fund consists of actual returns and actual weights.

The fully restrained fund (sometimes called the "fully notional fund") represents the return on the policy portfolio—that is, the strategic benchmark or policy weights set by the asset owner (represented by the pension fund trustee) multiplied by the market index returns for each asset class. In mathematical notation,

$$b = \sum_{i=1}^{i=n} W_i \times b_i, \tag{5}$$

where:

W_i = weight of the benchmark in the ith asset class (note $\sum_{i=1}^{i=n} W_i = 1$)
b_i = return of the index in the ith asset class

The partly restrained fund (sometimes called the "semi-notional fund") represents the intermediate return resulting from the actual weights determined by the manager multiplied by the market index returns. Again, in mathematical notation,

$$b_S = \sum_{i=1}^{i=n} w_i \times b_i, \tag{6}$$

where w_i is the weight of the portfolio in the ith asset class (note $\sum_{i=1}^{i=n} w_i = 1$).

The actual portfolio return in mathematical notation is

$$r = \sum_{i=1}^{i=n} w_i \times r_i, \tag{7}$$

where r_i is the return of the portfolio assets in the ith asset class.

The performance of a fund—in this case, a pension fund—thus depends on two factors: the selection of asset classes (typically, now described as asset allocation) and the selection of securities within an asset class. (As noted earlier, this analysis can also be applied to sector allocation and stock selection within sectors in an exactly parallel way.) The contribution of each of these components can be found by breaking down the transition from the actual fund to the fully restrained fund as shown in **Table 1**.

Table 1. Source of Profit/Loss

Selection of asset classes (asset allocation)	Partly restrained fund minus fully restrained fund
Selection of securities	Actual fund minus partly restrained fund
Total	Actual fund minus fully restrained fund

The success of the manager's asset allocation is measured by comparing the performance of the partly restrained fund with that of the fully restrained fund. The success of the manager's security selection is measured by comparing the performance of the actual fund with that of the partly restrained fund.

The SIA (1972) report is thus crucial because it introduces the concepts of macro and micro levels of manager decision making and intermediate notional portfolios to calculate these effects.

In "Investment Performance of Pension Funds" (Holbrook 1977), the British actuary J.P. Holbrook, in effect, pulled together the BAI (1968) report, Fama's (1972) decomposition, and the SIA (1972) report. This virtually unknown paper provides the foundation for much of the development in performance analysis that followed. Directing his advice to pension fund trustees, Holbrook defined the decision-making process as follows:

> The practical management of a pension fund investment portfolio involves decisions at three levels.
>
> i) Policy, i.e. the proportions of the assets which, as a long-term aim, the trustees wish to hold in the different investment markets. The fundamental element of policy is the split between equity-type and fixed-interest investments. Definition of policy may extend to a split of equity-type investments between UK equities, overseas equities and properties, specific proportions being set for each. If the trustees are not experts in long-term investment, they will tend to formulate policy in discussion with specialist advisers; it is gratifying to record that actuaries who advise on the financing of pension schemes are increasingly becoming involved in such discussions.
>
> ii) Strategy, i.e. decisions to depart from the policy proportions in the light of current market conditions, including decisions to hold part of the fund on short-term deposit. The trustees will usually seek advice from experts in the various markets regarding the short-term outlook, up to the time of the next investment meeting and over the next year or so. Except where trustees delegate strategic decisions to managers and advisers, investment meetings are usually held at short regular intervals, and arrangements are made for special meetings whenever it is thought that there has been a material change in market prospects. Often trustees authorize the managers concerned to determine the timing of purchases; thus, a manager is able to retain part of the assets entrusted to him in the form of short-term deposits.

iii) Selection, i.e. the choice of the particular investments to hold, buy or sell within the various markets. Again, practice varies; many trustees give their managers carte blanche in this area— some keep close control over day-to-day transactions. (p. 20)

Holbrook went on to describe the trustees' needs. First, they need to know whether the fund performed well, moderately, or badly. This knowledge requires the calculation of return, comparisons with market returns, and consideration of risk:

> The performance of the fund as a whole, and within the different markets and sectors, must be examined separately. Secondly, the trustees need to be advised on the reasons for their fund's performance; this may be investigated by analysing the results to show contributions to total performance made by policy, strategy, and selection decisions. Finally, the trustees need help in interpreting the results as a guide to future action. Identification of points of strength and weakness in past performance may lead to reconsideration of policy and practice, of the decision-making process, and possibly to a change of manager. (p. 21)

To facilitate the breakdown of returns into policy, strategic, and selection decisions, Holbrook suggested the return calculation of three notional funds:

r_m = based on the model,
r_p = based on the trustees' policy proportions, and
r_A = based on actual allocations.

Then, the geometric excess return, g, for the whole fund is given by

$$(1+g)=\frac{(1+r)}{(1+r_m)}=\frac{(1+r_p)}{(1+r_m)}\times\frac{(1+r_A)}{(1+r_p)}\times\frac{(1+r)}{(1+r_A)}. \tag{8}$$

> The first factor represents the contribution to total performance resulting from the decision to adopt a policy that differs from the equity and fixed-interest proportions in the model [the industry standard allocation between equity and fixed income at the time]. The second, the contribution from the strategic decision to depart from policy proportions. The third, the contribution from selection decisions for the fixed-interest and equity sectors taken together. (Holbrook 1977, p. 31)

This passage is the first articulation of successive notional portfolios each of which isolates one step in the investment decision process. The fact that it was written in 1977 shows how far ahead of his time Holbrook was.

Holbrook (1977) linked this successive notional portfolio approach to Fama's decomposition by equating the first factor to the investor's return from systematic risk, the second factor to the manager's return from systematic risk, and the third factor to selectivity.

Foundations

The Brinson Model. The next major development in attribution analysis stems from a series of papers written in the 1980s that collectively describe Brinson attribution.

Brinson, Hood, and Beebower's (1986) "Determinants of Portfolio Performance" is perhaps the most well-known paper on attribution. It provided the name for the most common type of equity attribution model used today: the Brinson model. Despite being a relatively short paper, it made two contributions:

1. The general framework used to decompose total portfolio returns. Brinson et al. (1986) suggested a model for breaking down the arithmetic return in excess of the benchmark $(r - b)$ under the assumption of a standard top-down investment decision process in which the portfolio manager seeks to add value through both *timing* and *security selection*. **Figure 2** illustrates their framework for analysing portfolio returns.

Quadrant I represents the policy benchmark return (b) for a period—that is, the return on a hypothetical portfolio wherein the asset-class weights are those in long-term investment policy (W_i) and the returns are those of the asset-class benchmarks (b_i).

$$\text{Quadrant I} = b = \sum_{i=1}^{i=n} W_i \times b_i. \quad (9)$$

Quadrant II represents the return effects of policy and timing.

In *timing*, the portfolio manager seeks to add value by holding asset-class (or sector) weights in the portfolio that are different from the asset-class benchmark weights. An asset-class weight in the portfolio that is greater than the benchmark weight for that asset class would be described as *overweight* and a lesser weight would be described as *underweight*. Clearly, the portfolio manager will aim to overweight well-performing asset classes (or sectors) and underweight poorly performing asset classes.

Quadrant II minus Quadrant I, therefore, describes the added or subtracted value from timing only.

Figure 2. The Brinson Quadrants

Allocation		Selection: Actual	Selection: Passive
	Actual	**Quadrant IV** Portfolio Return $r = \sum_{i=1}^{i=n} w_i \times r_i$	**Quadrant II** Policy & Timing $b_S = \sum_{i=1}^{i=n} w_i \times b_i$
	Passive	**Quadrant III** Policy & Selection $r_S = \sum_{i=1}^{i=n} W_i \times r_i$	**Quadrant I** Policy $b = \sum_{i=1}^{i=n} W_i \times b_i$

Excess returns due to:

Timing	II – I
Security Selection	III – I
Other	IV – III – II + I
Total	IV – I

Source: Brinson et al. (1986).

Quadrant III represents returns resulting from policy and security selection combined. In *security selection*, the portfolio manager seeks to add value by selecting individual securities within the asset class or sector.

Quadrant III minus Quadrant I, therefore, describes the added or subtracted value from selection only.

Quadrant IV represents the actual return of the managed portfolio.

Brinson et al. (1986) called the remaining term "other" or the "cross-product" term. It is now more commonly considered to be "interaction."

Quadrant IV minus Quadrant III minus Quadrant II plus Quadrant I represents the added or subtracted value from *interaction*.

2. In a more controversial practice, the framework is used on a sample of pension funds to demonstrate that most of the difference in returns among pension funds is the result of policy decisions, not timing or selection. This use of the framework is responsible for much of its fame.

Attribution Formulas. Brinson et al. (1986) may be the better known of the "Brinson papers," but the more important paper in terms of the development of attribution is "Measuring Non-US Equity Portfolio Performance" by Brinson and Fachler (1985). Again, it is a short paper, but it documented for the first time the formulas required to calculate individual attribution effects:

- *Allocation (Brinson and Fachler [1985] used the term "market selection").* The contribution to excess return from asset allocation in the ith sector is

$$A_i = (w_i - W_i) \times (b_i - b). \tag{10}$$

- *Selection.* The contribution to excess return from stock selection in sector i is

$$S_i = W_i \times (r_i - b_i). \tag{11}$$

- *Interaction (Brinson and Fachler used the term "cross-product").* The contribution to excess return from interaction in sector i is

$$I_i = (w_i - W_i) \times (r_i - b_i). \tag{12}$$

With a few modifications, these formulas provide the basic foundations for most of the attribution analysis used today. The terms "asset allocation," "security selection," and "interaction" are now universal and familiar to all. At the time, however, allocation might have been described as "timing," "market selection," or "weighting." To establish when the term "allocation" was first used is difficult, but Cocks (1972) was among the first. He defined it as "all those decisions by which the portfolio manager allocates his funds among the selected securities (or broad classes of securities)" (p. 3). *Asset allocation* specifically locates the decision process in what asset classes to hold and in what weights, and this terminology is associated with Ibbotson and Sinquefield (1982), although no one knows when the term was first used.

Use of the term "interaction" (or "other" or "cross-product") is difficult to establish, but certainly, by the early 1990s, "asset allocation," "security selection," and "interaction" had become the most commonly used terms.

The Brinson et al. (1986) paper did not provide a formula for individual attribution effects, but the following variation of the allocation formula is associated with that paper:

The contribution to excess return from asset allocation in the ith sector is

$$A_i = (w_i - W_i) \times b_i. \tag{13}$$

It seems unlikely that Brinson et al. (1986) intended this interpretation, and the Brinson and Fachler (1985) variant for asset allocation is far more common and better aligned with most investment decision processes. If the Brinson et al. definition is used, the contribution from asset allocation will be positive for any overweight sector in which the sector return is positive, but it will be positive when using the Brinson–Fachler definition only if the sector return exceeds the overall benchmark return.

Graphically, the Brinson et al. (1986) method is easier to illustrate for each sector i than the Brinson and Fachler (1985) method, as shown in **Figure 3**. The contribution to portfolio return from sector i is the total area $r_i \times w_i$, and the contribution from the benchmark alone is area $b_i \times W_i$. In this example the total contribution from the portfolio in sector i is greater than the contribution from the benchmark.

The attribution to excess return in sector i is the sum of the areas representing selection $[W_i \times (r_i - b_i)]$, allocation $[(w_i - W_i) \times b_i]$, and interaction $[(w_i - W_i) \times (r_i - b_i)]$. In this particular example, $r_i > b_i$, $b_i > 0$ and $w_i > W_i$; therefore, all three contributions are positive.

The Brinson and Fachler (1985) method illustrated in **Figure 4** is a little less intuitive. As stated in Bacon (2008), "We observe no change to the areas representing selection and interaction but allocation is now described by the area $(w_i - W_i) \times (b_i - b)$" (p. 125).

Figure 3. Brinson, Hood, and Beebower (1986) Attribution

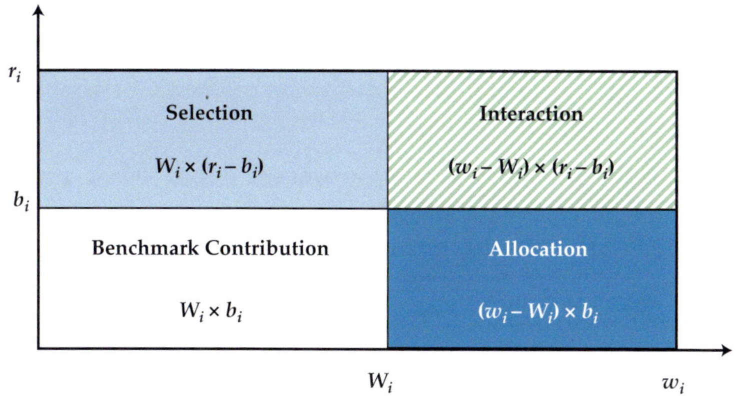

Source: Bacon (2008).

Figure 4. Brinson and Fachler Attribution

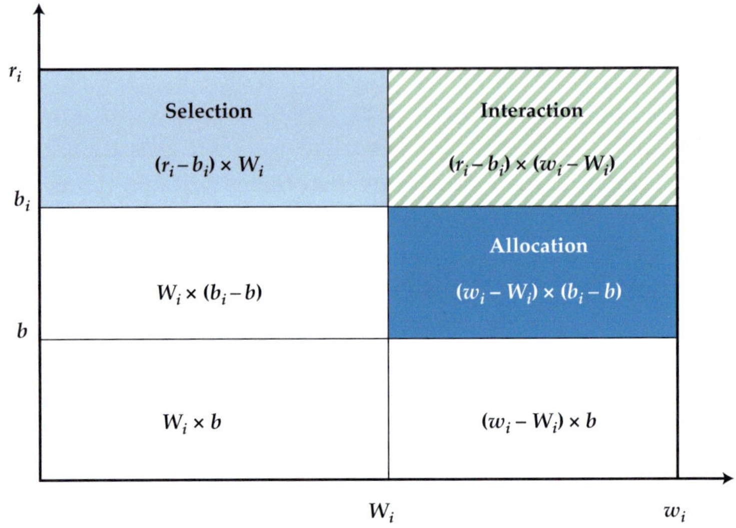

Source: Bacon (2008).

The traditional formulas described in Brinson and Fachler (1985) were clearly in use well before 1985. The same formulas as those suggested by Brinson–Fachler and associated with Brinson et al. (1986) can be found in a formal discussion response to a paper by Kingston (1973) presented to the Faculty of Actuaries on 14 October 1974, more than 10 years before the Brinson–Fachler paper was published.

The formulas may well have been developed prior to the publication of the Brinson and Fachler (1985), Brinson, Hood, and Beebower (1986), Brinson, Singer, and Beebower (1991), and Singer (1996) papers, but collectively these papers established attribution analysis as an important aid in the critical review of active strategies and decision-making processes for asset managers, asset consultants, and asset owners.

Interaction. Interaction is a controversial effect. Most authors—for example, Laker (2001), Spaulding (2003/2004), Campisi (2004b), and Bacon (2008)—would agree that the interaction effect is a directly calculated term, not a residual, but what does it mean? . . . It is certainly not intuitive. As noted, Brinson and Fachler (1985) and Brinson, Hood, and Beebower (1986), arguably the first definers of the interaction effect, rather unhelpfully described this effect as "other" or a "cross-product"; they did not use the term "interaction." By the early 1990s, the term had become fairly universal in the literature, however, probably popularised by the software providers of the time. The interaction effect is clearly a cross-product, the combination of allocation and selection decisions.

Laker (2000) suggested "that when calculated properly, the interaction term plays a valuable role in explaining a portfolio's active performance, and indeed that sometimes it is clearly more explanatory than the other attributes" (p. 43). Spaulding (2003/2004) was more nuanced in his comments, despite pointing out potentially misleading results (from mispriced securities or investing in sectors not in the benchmark). On balance, Spaulding suggested, it is best to calculate interaction, take the time to do some analysis, and then decide where to assign it, or better yet, show the interaction as a separate item and prepare to explain it. Campisi (2004b) and Bacon (2008) were less supportive of using the interaction effect; they suggested that it is not an active part of the investment decision process and, therefore, need not be calculated. Like many asset managers in practice, they suggested including interaction in the selection effect.

The decision to include interaction with stock selection is not arbitrary. If you assume that asset allocation decisions are taken first in a top-down investment process, then the attribution from stock selection can be derived from Quadrant IV minus Quadrant II in Figure 2 and interaction need not be calculated at all. The decision to include interaction with stock selection is, therefore, the direct result of the investment decision process.

The contribution to stock selection in the *i*th sector is now

$$S_i = w_i \times (r_i - b_i), \qquad (14)$$

and Figure 4 can now be redrawn as shown in **Figure 5** with selection represented by the area $w_i \times (r_i - b_i)$.

Multiperiod Analysis

The attribution models described so far work well for single periods with static data. No obvious way exists, however, to combine attribution effects over time. Because of the multiplicative (geometric) nature of returns, arithmetic excess returns fail to add up over multiple periods. Carino (1999, p. 5) eloquently explained the problem this way:

> Over multiple periods, the natural way to combine returns is to compound them. The compounded return R over t periods is
>
> $$R = (1 + r_i) \times (1 + r_2) \times \cdots \times (1 + r_t) - 1. \qquad [15]$$

Figure 5. Selection including Interaction

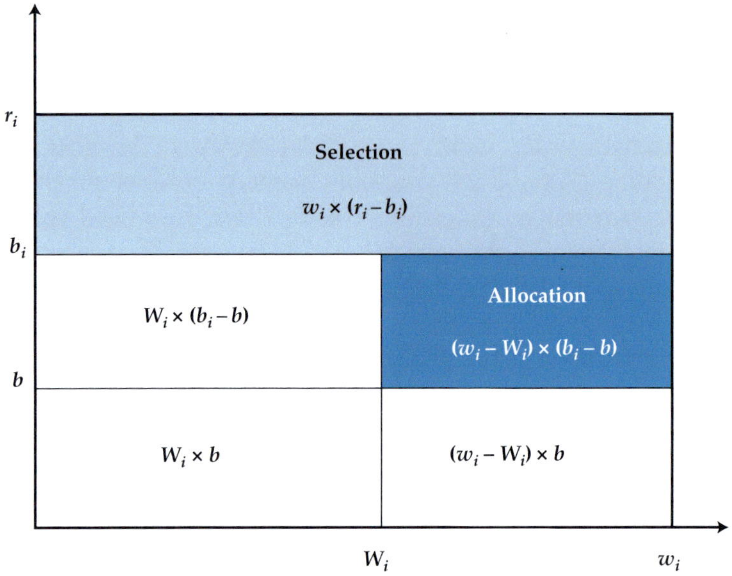

Source: Bacon (2008).

And for the benchmark,

$$B = (1+b_i)\times(1+b_2)\times\cdots\times(1+b_t)-1. \quad [16]$$

It is clearly unsatisfactory to simply add effects over time, because the sum of return differences does not equal the difference between compounded returns.

Singer (1996, p. 54) made the same point:

While it is tempting to simply add the individual periods to obtain multiperiod attribution results, it is wrong:

$$R - B \neq (r_i - b_i) + (r_2 - b_2) + \cdots + (r_t - b_t). \quad [17]$$

Nor is it satisfactory to compound the single period return differences because that result does not equal the difference in compounded returns either.

Laker (2002) made the point through this equation:

$$R - B \neq (1 + r_1 - b_1)\times(1 + r_2 - b_2)\times\cdots\times(1 + r_t - b_t) - 1. \quad (18)$$

Linking and Smoothing. Obviously, if multiperiod arithmetic excess returns do not add up, then clearly arithmetic attribution that adds up for single periods will not add up for multiple periods. Value added through active management decisions compounds over time, a fact that should be accounted for in multiperiod frameworks. Naturally, the end users of attribution analyses expect their analyses to add up without residuals.

Solutions can be categorized into two types, *smoothing algorithms*, such as those described by Carino (1999) and Menchero (2000), and *linking algorithms* (sometimes described as "dollar attribution"), such as those in GRAP (1997), Frongello (2002a, 2002b), and Bonafede, Foresti, and Matheos (2002).[1]

The authors of each paper suggested that their method was the most appropriate to implement. Smoothing algorithms, in effect, take the resulting residual and methodically redistribute it across other factors. Carino (1999) used logarithms, and Menchero (2000) redistributed the residual in an optimised way that minimised the change in any single factor. GRAP (1997), Frongello (2002a, 2002b), and Bonafede et al. (2002) compounded attribution effects through time and achieved identical results, but crucially, their methods are order dependent: If the time periods are reversed, the attribution result will change. Frongello acknowledged the order dependence but regarded it as a strength; others, including Laker (2002), would describe it as a weakness.

Davies and Laker (2001) suggested an "exact" method for using the Brinson model to calculate attributes over multiple periods at a portfolio level, but not sector level. Because of the so-called exact nature of their model, they suggested it would be helpful to evaluate the accuracy of other proposed methods by comparison with their method at the total portfolio level. Many articles have been written critiquing and defending existing methods and offering refinements and new methods, including Banchik (2004/2005), Carino (2002), David (2012/2013), Frongello (2002a, 2002b), Jiang and Saenz (2014/2015), Kirievsky and Kirievsky (2000, 2004), Laker (2002, 2005), Menchero (2003), Mirabelli (2000/2001), Reztsov (2011/2012), Spaulding (2002), and Wong (2003/2004, 2007). By and large, however, the end user has proven to be unconcerned about these black box approaches, provided that the multiperiod arithmetic attribution adds up without residuals. Frongello (2006) concluded that "although the mathematics can differ greatly from one method to another, the story told by the resulting attribution is the same regardless of the method" (p. 366).

[1]Software providers have typically found solutions but often keep their methods more or less proprietary.

Geometric Attribution. Some would suggest that the problem with multiperiod attribution analysis stems from an incorrect definition of excess return itself. Bacon (2002) defined the arithmetic excess return $(r-b)$ as the profit in excess of the notional fund expressed as a percentage of the initial value of the portfolio. That work defined the geometric excess return, $[(1+r)/(1+b)]-1$, as the profit in excess of the notional fund expressed as a percentage of the final value of the notional fund. In other words, the geometric excess return measures the added value in terms of a percentage of the value of the notional fund assets at the end of the period, not the start, which is surely the main concern of any asset owner.

Bacon (2002) suggested that geometric excess returns are preferable because they are compoundable (geometric excess returns compound over multiple periods without residuals), they are convertible among currencies, and they are proportionate. The preferred definition of excess return should determine the choice of attribution methodology. Bain (1996), Burnie, Knowles, and Teder (1998), and Bacon (2002) each presented a geometric attribution model. Although developed independently and presented in different ways, the models are, in fact, identical, which is an indication of the robustness of the approach. Geometric models built on the idea of successive notional portfolios can be found in Holbrook (1977), Hymans and Mulligan (1980), and Allen (1991). As shown in **Figure 6**, each successive portfolio

Figure 6. Successive Notional Portfolios

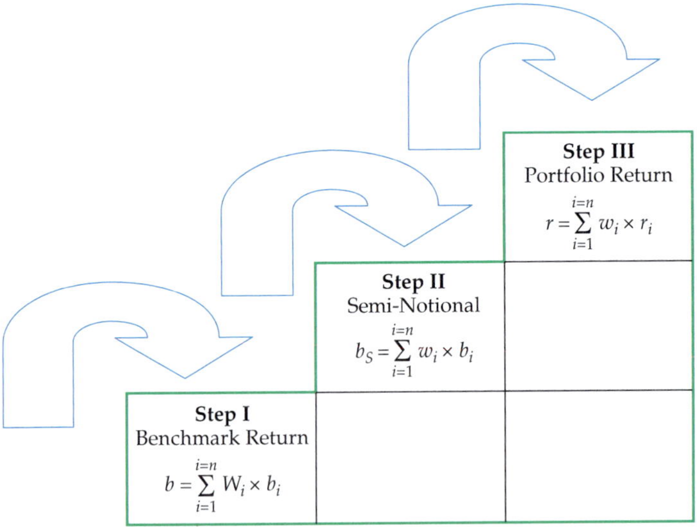

Source: Bacon (2008).

represents an isolated decision in a top-down investment decision process. Step I represents the strategic, policy, or benchmark return. The difference between Step II and Step I represents the value added by active asset allocation, and the difference between Step III and Step II represents the value added by security selection. More steps can be introduced for more complex, multistep investment decision processes.

In the geometric attribution model, the difference between each step is calculated geometrically:

$$\frac{(1+r)}{(1+b)}-1=\underbrace{\frac{(1+b_S)}{(1+b)}}_{\text{Allocation}}\times\underbrace{\frac{(1+r)}{(1+b_s)}}_{\text{Selection}}-1. \tag{19}$$

Because geometric excess returns compound through time and because geometric allocation effects and geometric selection effects compound together *within* each period, geometric allocation and geometric selection must also compound *through time*. Bain (1996), Burnie et al. (1998), and Bacon (2002) provided formulas for individual attribution effects as follows:

- *Allocation.* The contribution to geometric excess return from asset allocation in the ith sector (A_i^G) is

$$A_i^G=(w_i-W_i)\times\left(\frac{1+b_i}{1+b}-1\right). \tag{20}$$

- *Selection.* The contribution to geometric excess return from stock selection in sector i (S_i^G) is

$$S_i^G=w_i\times\frac{(r_i-b_i)}{(1+b_S)} \tag{21}$$

or

$$S_i^G=w_i\times\left(\frac{1+r_i}{1+b_i}-1\right)\times\frac{(1+b_i)}{(1+b_S)}. \tag{22}$$

In geometric attribution, interaction is typically included in the selection effect, although a geometric interaction effect can be derived if desired (see Weber 2018).

Burnie et al. (1998) described perhaps the most well-known geometric methodology. Interestingly, they made the case for geometric attribution in a single-period context, not necessarily a multiperiod one. They also drew a distinction between top-down and bottom-up investment decision processes. A bottom-up investment decision process, they noted, assumes that security selection takes precedence over asset allocation or is performed first.

Weber (2018) would consider the Bain (1996), Burnie et al. (1998), and Bacon (2002) models to be semi-geometric models. The reason is that although total selection and allocation effects compound to the geometric excess return, the effects within selection and allocation are still arithmetically calculated. Menchero (2001/2002) offered a fully geometric model in which individual selection and allocation effects compound through time.

Multicurrency Attribution

In this section, we consider three works specifically directed to performance attribution in currency management.

Allen (1991). In an article entitled "Performance Attribution for Global Equity Portfolios," Allen took the Holbrook (1977) concept of successive intermediate portfolios and applied it in a multicurrency environment. Allen stated that the trick to quantifying the impact of each type of active management decision involved calculating the return on a theoretical portfolio where one type of decision had been neutralised. Comparison of the return on the manager's portfolio (where no decisions had been neutralised) with the return on the portfolio where a class of management decisions had been neutralised allowed the impact of those neutralised decisions to be measured.

When carried out correctly, this process is quite neat. No unexplained residuals remain. Allen's article provides a framework for quantifying the marginal impact that both policy decisions and active management decisions have on the performance of a global equity portfolio. At the heart of this framework is the assumption that the total return on an actively managed global equity portfolio is explained by seven types of decisions:

1. the choice, at the policy level, of the unhedged dollar-denominated index against which the active equity manager is to be measured
2. security selection decisions by the active manager within each country
3. overweighting or underweighting of a country relative to the index based on the manager's expectation of the country's equity returns
4. overweighting or underweighting of a country relative to the index based on the manager's expectation of the country's currency returns

5. the timing of purchases and sales of securities (which implicitly affect the currency appreciation of the portfolio)
6. the choice, at the policy level, of the benchmark percentage of the portfolio that is to be hedged passively against currency fluctuation
7. active decisions in the currency forward markets that cause the portfolio's return to deviate from that of the passively hedged benchmark

Allen's article is noteworthy in that despite being based in the United States where arithmetic attribution prevails, he favored a geometric approach because the attribution factors are computed on a multiplicative basis, so they can be "chain-linked" across any time period to generate a cumulative factor. This method allows for evaluation of the long-term contribution of a selected investment strategy to total return.

Ankrim and Hensel (1992, 1994). In 1992, Ankrim and Hensel published a Russell Research Commentary setting out a framework for multicurrency performance attribution. This article, building on work by Brinson and Fachler (1985), separated out the impact of currency decisions—in particular, it recognised the significance of differential interest rates in currency decision making. Ankrim and Hensel proposed

> a method of performance attribution that retains the simplicity and intuitive appeal of the Brinson and Fachler approach but breaks the returns from currency into two components: one that recognizes the opportunity cost of returns achievable in forward-currency markets and a second that measures the return attributable to the currency being less than fully hedged, both in the portfolio and in the benchmark with which the portfolio is compared. (p. 2)

In the 1992 paper, Ankrim and Hensel identified three reasons that including currency exposure in performance attribution causes problems:

> First, and most obvious, it alters the returns ultimately received by the client. In Brinson and Fachler [1985], all returns are denominated in the home currency, but this convention makes it impossible to separate the contribution to returns made by the manager's country and security selection decisions from the impact of currency translation gains and losses.
>
> Second, in practice, many portfolios have some portion (but not necessarily all) of their currency exposure hedged away. This requires an approach to performance attribution that allows the proportion of currency exposure hedged to be variable.
>
> Third, even if a portfolio is completely hedged, the client may choose to adopt a benchmark that is less than fully hedged. (p. 2)

The authors defined two components of currency return: *currency surprise* and the *forward premium*. Currency surprise is uncertain, but the forward premium element is not because it depends on interest rate differentials at the time of purchase:

> Any approach to multicurrency attribution that lumps the forward premium and currency surprise together will credit positive performance to managers who have large exposures in countries with positive forward premiums. Such an approach would penalize managers who hold large positions in countries with negative forward premiums. (p. 12)

Karnosky and Singer (1994). Arguably the single most important paper published on attribution in the 1990s is Karnosky and Singer. This paper not only demonstrates that managing multicurrency portfolios is sub-optimal if currency is not managed independently but also provides a framework for calculating attribution effects, while critically, taking into account interest rate differentials. Karnosky and Singer resolved the issue of market and currency compounding by using continuously compounded returns in their model, admittedly this is only referred to in the small print, and solved the forward premium concern by thinking in terms of a "return premium" above local interest rates. Karnosky and Singer explained that the term "return premium" is used, rather than the more familiar "risk premium," to make a subtle distinction in the underlying cash return. "Risk premium" refers to the return of a risky asset in excess of the return of a riskless asset, but in the authors' analysis, the premiums depend on forward contracts with long maturities, where risk is probably not the dominant factor; hence, the term "return premium" is used.

Karnosky and Singer's framework demonstrates that separate currency and market strategies can be implemented within a global portfolio in which a specific currency weight is different from the weight of the associated country market. In effect, the authors applied the standard Brinson methodology twice—once to global portfolios by using local-return premiums (rather than simply local returns) to measure allocation and selection effects and, separately, to cash returns in the base currency of the asset owner in order to calculate independent currency effects, as shown in **Figure 7**.

Figure 7. Karnosky and Singer (1994) Multicurrency Attribution

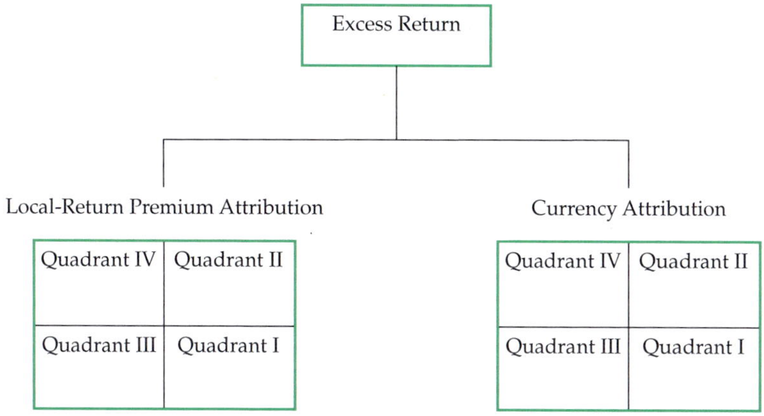

Source: Bacon (2008).

Types of Attribution

Three types of attribution have been identified, and they are characterized by the information used to calculate attribution effects, as follows:

1. Holdings-based attribution.

   Holdings-based or position-based attribution is calculated by analysing the underlying beginning-period holdings of the portfolio only. Typically, holdings-based attribution is calculated from monthly, weekly, or daily data, with the shorter time periods leading to greater accuracy.

2. Transaction-based attribution.

   Transaction-based attribution is calculated by using both the holdings of the portfolio and the transactions (purchases and sales) that occurred during the evaluation period.

3. Returns-based attribution.

   Returns-based (or factor) attribution uses the historical returns of the total portfolio and/or individual securities to decompose the total return into multiple factors. The multifactor model is a regression equation that describes the way a particular security or portfolio reacts to industry sector, fundamental, macroeconomic, and other market factors.

Asset-Grouping Attribution. The type of attribution favoured by the asset manager or asset owner will vary according to the investment decision process, investment objective, quality and availability of data, cost and time considerations, complexity, and reporting objective. Holdings-based and transaction-based attributions are mutually exclusive, and the choice is based on (for holdings based) cost, quality of data, ease of use, and rapid implementation against (for transaction based) the advantages of reconciliation to the client-reported return, completeness, and accuracy. A number of authors—Giguere (2003), Bonafede and McCarthy (2003), Spaulding (2003a), Menchero and Hu (2003), and Bacon (2008)—argued for one approach or another. Spaulding, without an eye to existing software (and thus genuinely independently), concluded that the question "which is better?" does not have a simple answer. Too many variables are at work; in the end, the choice comes down to user preference. In later research, Spaulding (2018) showed that the residual implicit in holdings-based attribution can be extensive and is not necessarily correlated with turnover. Both holdings-based and transaction-based attribution are also described as "asset-grouping" or "variance type" attribution, reflecting their requirements for asset allocation data and variance from benchmark data.

Attribution Based on Returns. Returns-based attribution, in contrast to the asset-grouping approach, might complement either holdings- or transaction-based attribution in that it might reveal unexpected biases and make communication easier for asset managers using a factor-focused investment decision process. Returns-based attribution is a direct descendant of Fama (1972) decomposition, which is a single-factor model, via Sharpe (1988) and Fama and French (1993)—both three-factor models that include a general market factor together with a size and value factor—and Carhart (1997), a four-factor model that introduced a momentum factor.

Amenc, Sfeir, and Martellini (2003) described four types of factor models:

1. Implicit factor model. In this model, some factor analysis (e.g., a principal components analysis) is performed to statistically extract the factors from the return's time series. These factors may not be easily interpretable.

2. Explicit macro factor model. In this approach, macroeconomic variables are used as factors.

3. Explicit micro factor model. In this approach, microeconomic attributes are used as factors.

4. Explicit index factor model. In this approach, stock market indexes (including style subindexes of the market) are used as factors.

Within this framework, Amenc and Le Sourd (2003) described a wide range of multifactor models in detail.

William F. Sharpe, who is associated with style attribution starting with his 1988 paper (see Sharpe 1988, 1992), used a 12-factor model to determine the passive return of a portfolio with the same style as the active asset manager. The difference between the actual portfolio return and the passive return with the same style would be a result of the manager's selection ability. This type of style analysis provides a natural method for constructing appropriate style benchmarks. Sharpe (1988) stated that the usefulness of the asset-class model depends on the asset classes chosen for implementation. It is desirable that asset classes

- be mutually exclusive,
- be exhaustive, and
- have returns that differ.

Each asset class should be proxied by a market capitalization–weighted index of the securities in it, and no security should be included in more than one asset class. Also, the asset classes should have low correlations with each other (or different standard deviations if correlations are high, as is the case in many fixed-income styles or asset subclasses).

Surz (1999/2000) suggested a holdings-based or transaction-based form of style attribution based on the exclusive style characteristics of the holdings in the portfolio and benchmark. Clarke, de Silva, and Thorley (2005) proposed a regression-based attribution system linked to the parameters from the "Fundamental Law of Active Management" (Grinold and Kahn 1995, pp. 117–35). In a slight oversimplification, the fundamental law says that alpha is a function of manager skill as well as breadth (the number of independent bets made by the manager). The investigation by Clarke et al. (2005) indicated that the "law can be used to estimate and interpret the regression-based results without substantial error while showing the investor how much of the active return is related to forecasting accuracy and how much is noise related to constraints in constructing the portfolio" (p. 81).

Returns-based or regression-based attribution has the following characteristics:

- It does not necessarily require the composition of the portfolio.
- It complements traditional holdings- or transaction-based attribution.
- It is relatively easy and cost-effective to implement.

- It is potentially most consistent with the investment decision process of the asset manager.
- It is easy to interpret.

However, this method does have limitations:

- It is less accurate than other methods, particularly for concentrated strategies.
- It relies on the appropriate definition of factors.

Risk-Adjusted Attribution

Campisi (2000) listed the characteristics of a good performance attribution system as follows:

- It is consistent with the investment process and the manager's decision-making process.
- It uses a benchmark that reflects the manager's strategic (long-term) asset allocation.
- It measures the effect of the manager's tactical (short-term) allocation shifts.
- It adjusts attribution of return for systematic risk(s).

Campisi (2000) suggested that many attribution systems fail at least one of these criteria and some fail all of them. Often, this failure occurs because returns are not adjusted for systematic risk and style (high vs. low beta, large vs. small size, value vs. growth orientation, etc.). Simply applying the allocation/selection model often results in attribution results that are not necessarily meaningful because they do not reflect the investment process or the risks that drove return over the evaluation period. Risk-adjusted attribution is the real Cinderella of attribution analysis: In practice, risk-adjusted attribution is rarely performed. Ankrim (1992) proposed a form of risk-adjusted attribution using beta, as did Bacon (2008) and Obeid (2005). Kophamel (2003), thinking in terms of the volume of "performance cubes" rather than the familiar "performance areas" of the Brinson model, proposed attribution analysis in three dimensions. Spaulding (2016) suggested adjusting for total risk rather than systematic risk—in effect, attributing M2 returns (described in Modigliani 1997).[2] Rather satisfactorily, Fisher and D'Alessandro (2019)

[2]Modigliani risk-adjusted performance (also known as M^2, M2, the Modigliani–Modigliani measure, or RAP) is a measure of the risk-adjusted returns of some investment portfolio. It measures the returns of the portfolio adjusted for the risk of the portfolio relative to that of some benchmark (e.g., the market).

took attribution full circle and tied risk-adjusted attribution back to the original Fama decomposition.

Van Breukelen (2000) suggested a form of risk-adjusted attribution for fixed-income portfolios that takes into account the weighted duration "bets" of portfolio managers. Van Breukelen described a top-down investment decision process in which overall duration is the first decision followed by a market allocation decision—a combination of country weight and duration—and finally, an issue selection decision within country. Currency effects are measured separately using a Karnosky and Singer (1994) type of approach. The value added by each step of the decision process is measured by using a series of reference or successive notional portfolios.

Fixed-Income Attribution

The simple Brinson model is widely regarded as being insufficient for all but the simplest of fixed-income investment strategies. McLaren (2002) explained that classical attribution models (e.g., Brinson's model) are inappropriate for fixed-income portfolio analysis because the allocation decision in equity models does not explicitly account for yield-curve positioning (duration) set by fixed-income managers. This omission is significant because the duration decision, which has no direct equity counterpart, plays an important role in the fixed-income decision-making process. Campisi (2000) also explained why fixed income needs its own attribution model and pointed out five critical differences between stocks and bonds:

1. Bonds are temporary lending agreements with a stated maturity, whereas stocks are permanent investments.
2. Bonds promise a fixed return, with a strictly defined upside if held to maturity; stocks promise uncertain returns and the unlimited upside (and downside) associated with ownership.
3. Bonds are typically purchased by institutions, which often hold them until maturity. This pattern results in a limited secondary market for bonds. Stock investing takes place in an active secondary market. As a result, bonds are illiquid compared with stocks.
4. Bond performance is driven by promised income and by changes in market yields: When market yields rise above a bond's stated yield, the price of that bond falls. As a result, the relevant risk for bonds is sensitivity to changes in yields. Stock performance is driven by the market's economic sectors, and the principal risks for stocks are (a) sensitivity to the overall market, or beta, and (b) the individual fortunes of the company invested in.

5. Bonds are simply the promise of a stream of cash flows; thus, they are relatively homogeneous in their pricing. For example, bonds with the same maturity and default risk will generally sell at the same price. Therefore, bonds reflect little selection effect. Stock prices, in contrast, respond dramatically to company-specific conditions and thus reflect a large selection effect.

Distinct approaches for fixed-income attribution emerged quite quickly in the early development of attribution. The method described in Wagner and Tito (1977) is derived directly from Fama decomposition, with beta replaced by a systematic risk measure for bonds—namely, duration. In this approach, fixed-income portfolio performance is driven by promised income and by the effect that changes in yields have on bond prices.

No single, standardised way of defining fixed-income attribution exists. The asset class has more securities than in equity investing, more types of instruments, more variety in investment process, and more quantitative modelling requirements. It also has various ways of describing change in the yield curve and a broad array of investment mandates. Murira and Sierra (2006) explained that each of the commercially available systems uses its own particular brand of return attribution. In fact, because of differences in the definition and computation of the factors, different systems often provide different values for the same return factor.

Other authors have made various contributions to developments in fixed-income attribution—developments often linked to specific investment decision processes or specific software capabilities. These authors include Ramaswamy (2001), Giguere (2005), Colin (2005, 2014), Gillet and Hommolie (2006), Colin, Cubilie, and Bardoux (2006), Silva, de Carvalho, and Ornelas (2010), Simmons and Karadakov (2013/2014), and Dias (2017).

Figure 8 illustrates the attribution effects in a typical fixed-income attribution model. Here, *carry* represents the return resulting from the passage of time: *coupon* payments, accrued interest, and *rolling down* the yield curve (the pull-to-par effect as the instrument approaches maturity).

In Figure 8, the *yield-curve* factor represents the changing shape of the yield curve, *parallel shift* (the impact of a parallel move of the yield curve), *twist* (a change in slope of the yield curve), and *curvature* (change in the curvature of the yield curve). Often, twist and curvature are combined and described as nonparallel changes in the yield curve or *curve reshape*.

Spread is the return that comes from the widening or narrowing of credit spreads.

Figure 8. Fixed-Income Attribution Effects

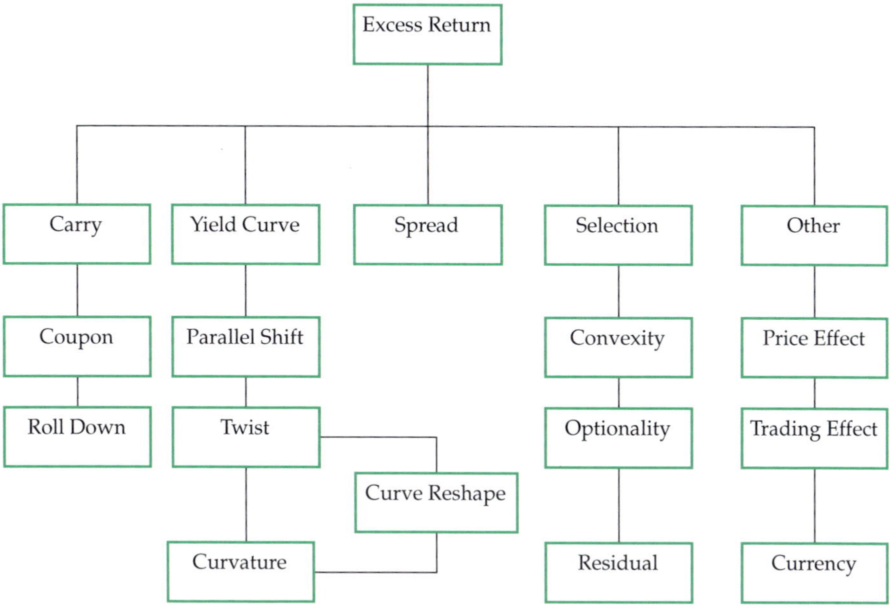

Source: Redrawn from a diagram in Dai and Elliot (2014/2015).

Selection effects include *convexity*, any *optionality* in the payment of future coupons (important with mortgage-backed securities because mortgages can be prepaid), and a *residual*. Normally quite small, residuals are classified by Dias (2017) as caused by the model or caused by data errors and systematic or random effects.

In the *other* category, the *price* effect captures the difference in price sources between the bonds in the portfolio and bonds in the benchmark. This is a nonmanagement effect that is a particular problem for fixed income. The *trading effect* measures the impact of intraday trading. *Currency* captures the impact of independent currency management, typically by using a Karnosky and Singer (1994) type of approach.

Fixed-income attribution models can be characterised as either top-down successive portfolio methods (e.g., Van Breukelen 2000) or bottom-up (yield-curve decomposition) methods. Bottom-up methods calculate the impact of yield-curve movements and credit spreads on individual bonds in both the portfolio and the benchmark and aggregate results. Top-down models are perhaps easier to implement and more effective in terms of communicating to asset owners and other stakeholders.

Gillet and Hommolie (2006) described the bottom-up approach as a successive spread methodology that can be split into two phases. The first phase consists of decomposing the bond prices into its various characteristics (passage of time, evolution of yield curves, variation of spreads). This decomposition is applied simultaneously to the constituents of the portfolio and to the constituents of the benchmark. The second phase consists only of regrouping the separated elements according to the investment decision process (p. 65). Bottom-up models are more difficult and expensive to implement but more appropriate to the detailed investment decision processes of the front office.

McLaren (2002) offered a geometric fixed-income attribution model, which is not common. Most fixed-income attribution models are arithmetic in nature, although for the most part, they can be adapted for geometric analysis. The reason may be that excess returns are typically smaller than in equity investing and the underlying benchmark returns less volatile, making the difference between geometric and arithmetic excess return smaller in magnitude.

Other Attribution Issues

Other issues in attribution pertain to derivatives, transaction costs, frequency of the analysis, and application to money-weighted returns.

Derivatives. The Brinson model is an incredibly robust methodology. Stannard (1997), Menchero (2002/2003), Bacon (2008), Fischer and Wermers (2013), and Bacon, Thompson, and van der Westhuizen (2018)—all described, using appropriate notional assets and notional returns, how the standard Brinson model can be adapted to handle derivative instruments, including index futures, options (of various types), and swaps and short positions.

Transaction Costs. Laker (2001) pointed out that transaction costs—explicit costs (such as brokerage and taxes) and implicit costs (such as the bid–offer spread, market impact, and opportunity cost)—are not dealt with explicitly in most performance attribution methods but are normally included within the stock selection effect. In a bottom-up, security-level attribution approach, Laker suggested using the standard Brinson selection formulas at the security level to calculate the impact of transaction costs (explicit and implicit) and intraday timing effects. He suggested that any return difference between an individual security's daily return and its return in the index must be the result of transaction costs and timing within the day.

Frequency of Analysis. DiBartolomeo (2003) challenged the assumption that aggregated daily attribution analysis is more appropriate than monthly aggregated analysis and suggested that applying typical attribution methods to daily data draws on assumptions that are highly biased and unreliable. Beyond simply observing the attributed returns, he believed, you must be able to judge their statistical significance. He suggested that recommending daily observation rests on four fallacies:

1. Daily performance is economically meaningful. Not necessarily—for example, information is lost by adjusting for the timing of cash flows in time-weighted returns.
2. Daily returns are themselves accurate. Not necessarily—many securities are traded on multiple exchanges or electronic markets at different times, so exactly which closing price is used to compute the daily returns can have a sizable impact. Also, coordinating the timing of corporate actions such as dividends, spin-offs, and mergers with index providers is difficult.
3. Observations are assumed to be independent. Investment portfolios do not start as a fresh set of management decisions every trading day. Thus the rationale of an independent "start fresh" assumption is weak. Substantial path dependencies are present in portfolio management in practice, which reduces any justification for the assumption of independent periodic observations of manager skill.
4. Parametric distributional assumptions are accurate. Most of the academic literature illustrates that the imperfections of our assumptions with respect to quarterly or monthly return data are small, whereas for daily data, we must consistently reject the correctness of the assumptions. In general, daily security returns have fat-tailed distributions, with large return events occurring far more often than would be consistent with a normal distribution. This issue is less of a problem with quarterly or monthly returns.

DiBartolomeo (2003) concluded that daily performance attribution compounds to a more accurate measure of the time-weighted return than attribution using less frequent data—but at a tremendous cost in our ability to judge the statistical significance of the results. Most of the imperfections of daily attributions result in upwardly biased confidence levels in our estimates of manager skill, leading to persistent Type 1 errors (believing an estimate is statistically significant when it is not).

Darling and MacDougall (2002/2003) certainly questioned the benefits of more frequent and more detailed performance measurement. They suggested that the cost of daily stock-level attribution is difficult to justify (although given recent developments in technology their views may have changed). They suggested that monthly modified Dietz calculations might actually be near the optimum balance and that a simple alternative might be running actual profit and loss for each position.[3]

Frongello (2006), in contrast, made the case for daily attribution analysis. He explained that in the real world, risk factor mismatches may occur unintentionally—caused by neglect, accidents, or simply changes in the risk profile of securities. Performance attribution should seek to explain performance resulting from all risk factor mismatches. Daily attribution is the best method for monitoring the status and consequence of risk factor mismatches (p. 367).

Zangari and Bayraktar (2005/2006) suggested that daily attribution, if done methodically, should produce results that are superior to monthly attribution. They pointed out that regardless of the methodology used, what is ultimately critical is the process governing attribution. The five core components of what they considered to be a good return attribution process are as follows:

1. Data management and quality control. This task is the most important. Positions, prices, corporate actions, and so on, must be accurately captured, processed, and incorporated.
2. Infrastructure. Without proper infrastructure (efficient application of hardware and databases), the chance of errors and delays increases.
3. Analytics. Algorithms perform the attribution calculations.
4. Methods. For example; daily buy-and-hold, monthly buy-and-hold, and transaction-based attribution.
5. Reports. The way in which information is presented is important, so timely, accurate, and easy-to-understand attribution reports are necessary.

Zangari and Bayraktar (2005/2006) concluded that process plays a critical part in determining the accuracy of attribution results. Return attribution should be based on a process that monitors key input data and evaluates attribution results on a daily basis.

Attribution of Money-Weighted Return. For purposes of comparative analysis, most attribution analysis is naturally undertaken on time-weighted rates of return (TWR). Attribution analysis of money-weighted rates of return (MWR) is less common. Yet, attribution analysis of MWR is still undertaken in the form of the modified Dietz return calculation method.

[3]The modified Dietz method is a mathematical technique to evaluate a portfolio's return based on a weighted calculation of its cash flow. The method takes into account the timing of cash flows and assumes a constant rate of return over a specified period of time.

It was, in fact, recommended by Menchero and Hu (2003) in the context of transaction-based attribution and by Darling and MacDougall (2002/2003). O'Shea and Jeet (2018) suggested single-period attribution of modified Dietz returns for private equity. Spaulding and Campisi (2007) made the case for money-weighted attribution. They suggested that because cash flow movements are a factor that defines the investment process, these cash flows must be part of the performance measurement and evaluation system instead of being neutralised (as occurs in the time-weighted calculation).

The modified Dietz method is a first-order approximation of the internal rate of return (IRR) and, according to Bacon (2007a), an intermediate step in the evolution from calculating IRR (which some might describe as a true MWR) to the true TWR. The IRR is a standard return measure for illiquid asset classes—such as private equity, real estate, and infrastructure—and is common at the total-asset owner level, where comparative analysis is less relevant. The modified Dietz method is easy to disaggregate and more straightforward to attribute than the IRR. Nevertheless, Illmer and Marty (2003) and Illmer (2009) offered a solution to the attribution of the true MWR in terms of both return and profit and loss.

D'Alessandro (2016) suggested analysts should end the debate about which method of return to use, TWR or MWR, and require the presentation of both with an attribution between the two.

Conclusion: The Evolution of Attribution Methodologies

The evolution of attribution analysis is clear, easy to trace, and illustrated in **Figure 9**, which maps, not necessarily in chronological order, the major developments in attribution analysis discussed in this review.

Comparative performance measurement starts with the BAI (1968) study, but attribution analysis itself starts with Fama (1972). From that point, a divergence occurs between asset-grouping and variance-type attribution, with the UK SIA (1972) introducing the concept of selection, allocation, and notional portfolios and return-based attribution developed a little later by Sharpe (1992), Fama and French (1993), Carhart (1997), and many others. Fixed-income attribution naturally veers in a different direction via Wagner and Tito (1977), who replaced beta with duration in the Fama decomposition, and Lord (1997), who responded to the investment decision processes of bond managers, which are so different from those of equity managers.

Very early, a split occurred between, on the one hand, the dominant arithmetic Brinson and Fachler (1985) and Brinson et al. model (1986) and, on the other hand, the total level geometric approach of Holbrook (1977). Smoothing and linking algorithms were soon needed in order for multiperiod

Figure 9. The Evolution of Attribution Methodologies

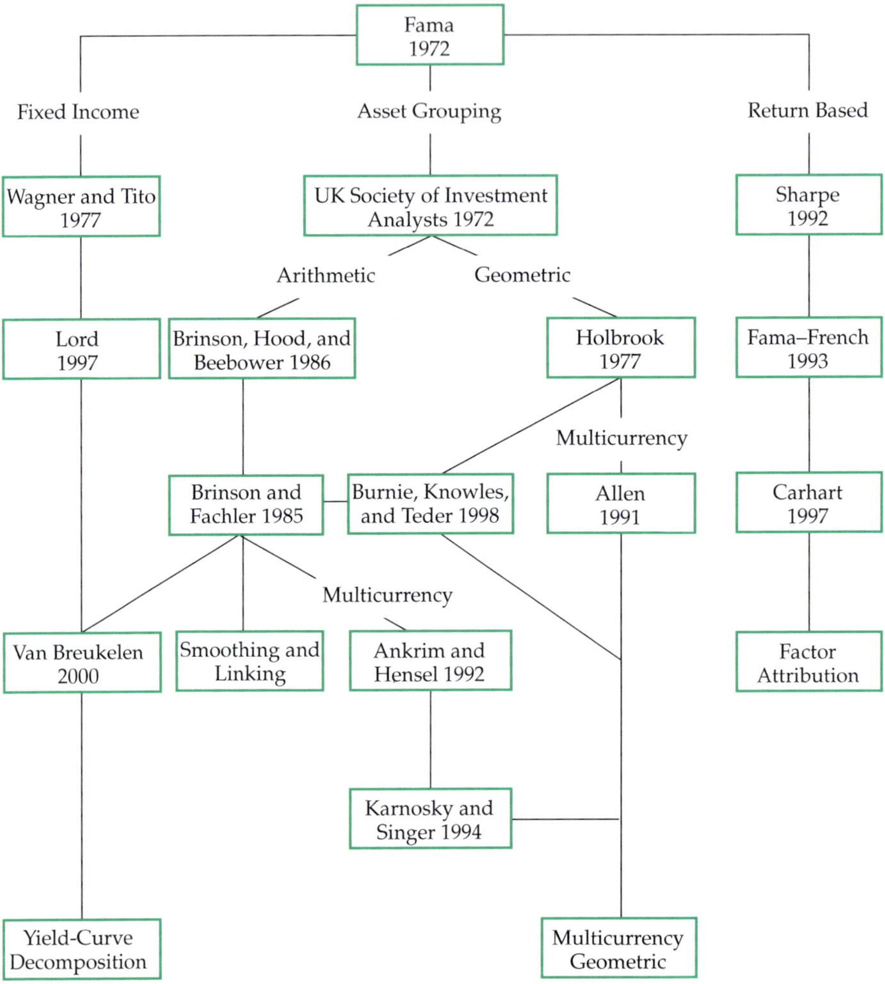

Source: Author.

arithmetic models to add up, which were, for the most part, designed and implemented by software firms to meet client requirements. Algorithms started to be published several years after their initial use in Carino (1999), soon followed by GRAP (1997), Menchero (2000), Frongello (2002a, 2002b), and Bonafede et al. (2002). Allen (1991) is a direct link from Holbrook but addressed multicurrency issues. Burnie et al. (1998), together with Bain (1996) and Bacon (2002), developed geometric selection and allocation calculations that were missing from Holbrook (1977) and from Allen. Ankrim and

Hensel (1992) and, with more success, Karnosky and Singer (1994) adapted the basic Brinson model for multicurrency attribution, including, importantly, taking into account interest rate differentials. Van Breukelen (2000) adapted the Brinson model for successive portfolio fixed-income attribution.

Figure 9 firmly cements Brinson and Fachler (1985) at the centre of developments in attribution analysis. In more recent years, we have seen many variants of yield-curve decomposition models, which reflects the diversity of fixed-income investment decision processes. Because of low uptake, risk-adjusted attribution is not illustrated here but could be represented by a link between return-based methods and the Brinson model.

Bibliography

Allen, Gregory C. 1991. "Performance Attribution for Global Equity Portfolios." *Journal of Portfolio Management* 18 (1): 59–65.

This article provides a framework for quantifying the marginal impact that both policy decisions and active management decisions have on the performance of a global equity portfolio. The article is noteworthy because, influenced by currency effects, it represents an early US-based example of geometric or multiplicative attribution; it emphasises the value of "no unexplained residuals" and attribution factors that "chain-link."

Amenc, Noel, and Veronique Le Sourd. 2003. *Portfolio Theory and Performance Analysis*. John Wiley & Sons.

This wide-ranging academic work evaluating the quality of the portfolio management process connects each of the major categories of techniques and practices to the unifying and seminal conceptual developments of modern portfolio theory. Of particular relevance to attribution analysis is Chapter 6 on multifactor models and their application to performance measurement, Chapter 7 on evaluating the investment management process and decomposing performance, and Chapter 8 on fixed-income security investment.

Amenc, Noel, Daphne Sfeir, and Lionel Martellini. 2003. "An Integrated Framework for Style Analysis and Performance Measurement." *Journal of Performance Measurement* 7 (4): 35–41.

This article explains that risk-adjusted performance evaluation consists of using a factor model to compare the overall performance of a manager with the "normal" performance the manager would get from being exposed to rewarded sources of risk. The article suggests the use of two important tools: (1) return-based style analysis, which allows the formation of peer groups of comparable managers, and (2) a customised multifactor model to estimate superior risk-adjusted performance (alpha) within each group.

Ankrim, Ernest M. 1992. "Risk-Adjusted Performance Attribution." *Financial Analysts Journal* 48 (2): 75–82.

The author suggests that classical attribution analysis does not consider risk and posits that in general, such methods will tend to overreward risky managers and underreward conservative ones. The author proposes an attribution approach that adjusts for the systematic risk of each sector.

Ankrim, Ernest M., and Chris R. Hensel. 1992. "Multi-Currency Performance Attribution." Russell Research Commentary (November).

Ankrim, Ernest M., and Chris R. Hensel. 1994. "Multicurrency Performance Attribution." *Financial Analysts Journal* 50 (2): 29–35.

These articles, both originally published in a Russell Research Commentary, expand the work of Brinson and Fachler (1985), separate out the impact of currency decisions, and, in particular, recognise the significance of differential interest rates in currency decision making.

Bacon, Carl R. 2002. "Excess Returns—Arithmetic or Geometric?" *Journal of Performance Measurement* 6 (3): 23–31.

This article sets out to define arithmetic and geometric excess returns. The author explains that the choice of an arithmetic or geometric attribution method is really a choice between using arithmetic or geometric excess return, and he expresses a preference for geometric excess returns based on compoundability, convertibility, and proportionality. Finally, the author presents a geometric attribution model that, although developed independently, is actually identical to that of Burnie, Knowles, and Teder (1998).

Bacon, Carl R. 2007a. "Money-Weighted versus Time-Weighted Attribution." *Journal of Performance Measurement* 11 (Performance Attribution Supplement): 21–27.

The author illustrates and explains the evolution of return calculations from internal rates of return to true time-weighted rates of return. In summary, the author suggests that time-weighted forms of attribution will remain dominant because of the following:

- The time-weighted rate of return is most appropriate for comparisons of managers.

- Internal rates of return assume a constant rate of return difficult to attribute.
- Investment decisions are independent of the total amount invested.
- Time-weighted attribution can measure the manager's timing decisions.
- Money-weighted attribution misallocates estimates of manager skill between stock selection and asset allocation.

Bacon, Carl R. 2007b. "Multi-Currency Attribution—Part 1: The Real Nature of Multi-Currency." *Journal of Performance Measurement* 12 (1): 22–29.

The author lists the issues of genuinely multicurrency investment decision processes:

- compounding effects of market and currency returns
- interest rate differentials
- unrealized gains/losses in forward currency contracts
- securities denominated in currencies other than the currency of economic exposure

Building on the work of Allen (1991), the author moves on to describe a naive form of currency attribution (naive in that it ignores currency differentials).

Bacon, Carl R. 2007/2008. "Multi-Currency Attribution—Part 2: Factoring in Interest Rate Differentials." *Journal of Performance Measurement* 12 (2): 8–19.

The author introduces the concepts of Karnosky and Singer (1994) into a geometric framework that takes full account of interest rate differentials.

Bacon, Carl R. 2008. *Practical Portfolio Performance Measurement and Attribution*. John Wiley & Sons.

This general book on performance analysis includes specific chapters on performance attribution, multicurrency attribution, fixed-income attribution, multiperiod attribution, and performance measurement for derivatives.

Bacon, Carl R. 2013. *Practical Risk-Adjusted Performance Measurement*. John Wiley & Sons.

This book documents with extensive references a large number of discrete ex-post risk measures and explains how they are related.

Bacon, Carl R., Ian Thompson, and Pierre van der Westhuizen. 2018. "Abnormal Returns." *Journal of Performance Measurement* 20 (3): 43–49.

The authors demonstrate the robustness of the Brinson–Fachler (1985) model for short positions.

BAI. 1968. *Measuring the Investment Performance of Pension Funds for the Purpose of Inter-Fund Comparison*. Bank Administration Institute.

The purpose of the BAI study, the starting point for performance analysis, was to develop methods of comparing the performance of pension funds in order to differentiate between the abilities of their respective managers. The report recommended, among other things, the use of market value, not book value; total return; time-weighted rates of return; and taking risk into account.

Bain, William G. 1996. *Investment Performance Measurement*. Woodhead Publishing.

This book is, for the most part, concerned with the measurement and analysis of pension fund investment portfolios. Most notable is its description of the WM Company's multiplicative (or geometric) attribution methodology (pp. 65–74).

Banchik, Sean. 2004/2005. "Pure and Inter-Period Interaction Effects in Multi-Period Attribution." *Journal of Performance Measurement* 9 (2): 53–63.

The author concludes that there is no single correct way to link single-period arithmetic effects to produce multiperiod effects. The appropriate methodology is generally one of personal preference. The most relevant question for the reader is not which method is correct but whether the reader understands where these effects are included in the chosen methodology.

Bonafede, Julia K., Steven J. Foresti, and Peter Matheos. 2002. "A Multi-Period Linking Algorithm That Has Stood the Test of Time." *Journal of Performance Measurement* 7 (1): 15–26.

The authors introduce a linking algorithm for multiperiod arithmetic attribution. The method was in use from the early 1980s, but this description was not published until 2002.

Bonafede, Julia K., and Mary Cait McCarthy. 2003. "Transaction-Based vs. Holdings-Based Attribution: The Devil Is in the Definitions." *Journal of Performance Measurement* 8 (1): 42–51.

The authors suggest that because full benchmark and portfolio valuation is not realistically available at each transaction time, true transaction-based performance attribution is not possible. Only buy-and-hold returns are consistent with benchmarking needs; therefore, performance attribution for portfolio management should use holdings-based return analysis. The authors propose an additional term called "trading" to explain the difference.

Brinson, Gary P., and Nimrod Fachler. 1985. "Measuring Non-US Equity Portfolio Performance." *Journal of Portfolio Management* 11 (3): 73–76.

This hugely important paper documented, for the first time, selection and allocation formulas at the sector level. The paper helped lend "Brinson" to the name of the most commonly used attribution model.

Brinson, Gary P., L. Randolph Hood, Jr., and Gilbert L. Beebower. 1986. "Determinants of Portfolio Performance." *Financial Analysts Journal* 42 (4): 39–44.

This extremely well-known paper is important for two reasons. First, it provided the general framework for the decomposition of portfolio return into selection, allocation, and interaction effects (although this last piece is described as "other" in the paper). Second, and more controversially, the paper made the observation that policy decisions make by far the biggest contribution to the differences in returns among pension funds.

Brinson, Gary P., Brian D. Singer, and Gilbert L. Beebower. 1991. "Determinants of Portfolio Performance II: An Update." *Financial Analysts Journal* 47 (3): 40–48.

This paper updated and confirmed the results first published in Brinson, Hood, and Beebower (1986).

Burnie, J. Stephen, James A. Knowles, and Toomas J. Teder. 1998. "Arithmetic and Geometric Attribution." *Journal of Performance Measurement* 3 (1): 59–68.

Most attribution models are arithmetically formulated and measure the manager's "value added"—or the difference between a fund's return and a passive benchmark return. The authors of this paper contended that such models are prone to error and may produce inconclusive results. This paper illustrates the benefits of using geometric attribution, which defines the "management effect" as the ratio of the fund return factor to the benchmark return factor.

This paper is of fundamental importance in addressing the relative advantage of geometric over arithmetic attribution, multiperiod attribution, and the ambiguity of the interaction or cross-product effects and defining top-down and bottom-up attribution.

Campisi, Stephen. 2000. "Primer on Fixed Income Performance Attribution." *Journal of Performance Measurement* 4 (4): 14–25.

The author explains that the drivers of fixed-income performance are fundamentally different from those of equity portfolios. Bond portfolio performance is driven by promised income and by the effect that changes in yields have on bond prices. The author proposes a simple attribution model that provides a straightforward method for identifying the systematic risk and stylistic factors of the asset manager's strategy.

Campisi, Stephen. 2004a. "The Case for Money-Weighted Performance Attribution." *Journal of Performance Measurement* 8 (3): 31–41.

The proposal in this paper is that although the case is irrefutable for accepting the time-weighted return as the preferred method for measuring the return of an asset manager, an equally compelling case can be made for accepting the money-weighted return as the appropriate method for evaluating the source of that active return; that is, the money-weighted return is the correct method for performance attribution.

Campisi, Stephen. 2004b. "Debunking the Interaction Myth." *Journal of Performance Measurement* 8 (4): 63–70.

The author refutes the idea of "interaction" and demonstrates that interaction arises from either a poor attribution model or a poor implementation of a sound attribution model. When a sound attribution model is implemented correctly, the interaction effect is eliminated. Despite the appearance of mathematical rigor in the calculation of interaction, investors and clients understand that interaction is not a legitimate part of the investment process.

Campisi, Stephen, and David Spaulding. 2007. *Readings in Fixed Income Performance Attribution*. TSG Publishing.

This book is a useful compendium of many of the articles included in this review.

Canty, Mike. 2017/2018. "Evolving Performance Attribution to Support Exploratory Excess Return Decomposition." *Journal of Performance Measurement* 22 (2): 27–38.

The author proposes three ways to improve arithmetic performance attribution. First, the total weight associated with the stock selection effect should exclude the asset allocation effect. Second, the assessment of an asset allocation decision should consider the actual returns connected to that decision. Third, excess return decomposition should exclude the impact of overlapping issue-level positions.

Carhart, Mark M. 1997. "On Persistence in Mutual Fund Performance." *Journal of Finance* 52 (1): 57–82.

In this highly influential paper, the author proposes an extension to the Fama–French (1993) three-factor model by adding a momentum factor.

Carino, David R. 1999. "Combining Attribution Effects over Time." *Journal of Performance Measurement* 3 (4): 5–14.

This paper discloses Frank Russell Company's method of combining attribution effects over time and displaying results in an additive manner. The paper is important in that it is the first time a software firm published its method for linking multiple-period attribution results without residuals, thus encouraging other firms to publish their in-house linking methodologies.

Carino, David R. 2002. "Refinements in Multi-Period Attribution." *Journal of Performance Measurement* 7 (1): 45–53.

The author offers a derivation of the dollar family of linking algorithms (see Frongello 2002a, 2002b; GRAP 1997; and Bonafede, Foresti, and Matheos 2002) and discusses further refinements whilst cautioning the performance analyst to balance complexity against practicality.

Clarke, Roger, Harindra de Silva, and Steven Thorley. 2005. "Performance Attribution and the Fundamental Law." *Financial Analysts Journal* 61 (5): 70–83.

The authors propose a regression-based attribution system linked to the parameters from the "Fundamental Law of Active Management" (Grinold and Kahn 1995). Their investigation indicates that the law can be used to estimate and interpret the regression-based results without substantial error while showing the investor how much of the active return is related to forecasting accuracy and how much is noise related to constraints in constructing the portfolio.

Cocks, Graham. 1972. "An Objective Approach to the Analysis of Portfolio Performance." *Investment Analyst* 34: 3–7.

The author argues that the primary purpose of portfolio analysis should be to provide the portfolio manager with information to help improve future performance. The objective of performance analysis should be to measure the various elements of performance that reflect the decisions involved in the investment process. The author then suggests that investment decisions may be classified in two ways: selection and allocation. This paper is one of the first to use the term "allocation."

Colin, Andrew M. 2005. *Fixed Income Attribution*. John Wiley & Sons.

This book, one of the few devoted to fixed-income attribution, explains the theory and practice of fixed-income attribution in detail. The author also shows how to reveal the effects of multiple investment decisions in fixed-income portfolios, including yield return, term structure effects, credit and liquidity effects, and others. The book contains both theoretical and practical information about fixed-income attribution, including the mathematics of attribution, yield-curve modelling, practical limitations, benchmarks, and presentation tools.

Colin, Andrew M. 2014. *Attribution in Finance*. Flametree Technologies.

This comprehensive book devoted to the subject of performance attribution is very much focused on all aspects of fixed-income attribution but includes equity attribution, currency attribution, and smoothing algorithms.

Colin, Andrew M., Mathieu Cubilie, and Frederic Bardoux. 2006. "A New Approach to the Decomposition of Yield Curve Movements for Fixed Income Attribution." *Journal of Performance Measurement* 10 (4): 18–28.

The authors discuss the most common ways to describe yield-curve movements: shift, twist, and curvature. Shift is a parallel movement of the curve across all maturities. Twist is a steepening or flattening of the curve, and curvature occurs when a curve becomes more or less humped. The authors suggest an approach to decomposing curve changes that circumvents the difficulties inherent in principal components analysis and model fitting.

Dai, Tianci, and Mark Elliot. 2014/2015. "Fixed Income Attribution with Carry Effect." *Journal of Performance Measurement* 19 (2): 7–18.

These authors propose a way to capture the true carry return. Typical fixed-income return decompositions attempt to include the carry return, but the return is usually (inadequately) approximated by yield. The authors argue that using an accurate calculation better isolates the effects of yield-curve shifts, shape, and position; spread changes; and other factors.

D'Alessandro, Joe. 2016. "Using Brinson Attribution to Explain Differences between Time-Weighted (TWR) and Money-Weighted (IRR) Returns." *Journal of Performance Measurement* 20 (4): 11–21.

The author recommends ending the debate about which method of return to use—time-weighted or money-weighted returns—and requiring the presentation of both with a comparison of, or attribution between, the two.

Darling, Robert, and Alastair MacDougall. 2002/2003. "Using Performance Statistics: Have Measurers Lost the Plot?" *Journal of Performance Measurement* 7 (2): 22–32.

The authors question the benefits of carrying out performance measurement that is more frequent than monthly or in more detail. They suggest that the cost of daily stock-level attribution is difficult to justify and argue that monthly modified Dietz calculations may actually be near the optimal balance. A simple alternative, they note, might be to run actual profit-and-loss data for each position.

David, Mark R. 2012/2013. "A Case for Arithmetic Attribution." *Journal of Performance Measurement* 7 (2): 26–38.

The author questions the advantages of geometric attribution, proportionality, convertibility, and compoundability and suggests an arithmetic money-based compounded notional approach based on Davies and Laker (2001).

Davies, Owen, and Damien Laker. 2001. "Multiple-Period Performance Attribution Using the Brinson Model." *Journal of Performance Measurement* 6 (1): 12–22.

The authors agree that multiperiod arithmetic attribution is difficult but suggest an exact method for calculating attributes over multiple periods in the Brinson model at the portfolio, not the sector, level. They further suggest that because of the exact nature of their model, evaluating the accuracy of other proposed methods would be helpful.

Davis, Ben, and Jose Menchero. 2010/2011. "Beyond Brinson: Establishing the Link between Sector and Factor Models." *Journal of Performance Measurement* 15 (2): 8–20.

The authors show that the classic Brinson model is a special kind of factor (return-based) attribution model. They also demonstrate how this factor model can be augmented with other factors, such as styles, to gain insight that would not be possible using the classic Brinson framework.

Dias, Joao S. 2017. "Residuals on Duration-Based Fixed Income Attribution." *Journal of Performance Measurement* 21 (4): 8–20.

The author usefully classifies residuals in fixed-income attribution that are the result of the model or data errors (including various types of data error) and considers whether these errors are systematic or random. The author also asks the important question, What is an acceptable residual?

DiBartolomeo, Dan. 2003. "Just Because We Can Doesn't Mean We Should." *Journal of Performance Measurement* 7 (3): 30–36.

This paper presents four fallacies about daily observation and concludes that daily performance attribution compounds to a more accurate measure of the time-weighted return but at a tremendous cost in the analyst's ability to judge the statistical significance of results. Most of the imperfections of daily attributions result in upwardly biased confidence levels in estimates of manager skill, leading to persistent Type 1 errors.

Dietz, Peter O. 1966. *Pension Funds: Measuring Investment Performance.* Graduate School of Business of Columbia University and Free Press.

This book fired the starting gun for comparative performance measurement and established the dominance of time-weighted rate of return as the measure. Performance analysis is referenced but considered to be beyond the scope of the book.

Eadie, Dugald. 1973. "A Practical Approach to the Measurement and Analysis of Investment Performance." *Investment Analyst* 37: 12–18.

The author offers an early practical demonstration of attribution analysis using the notional fund concept.

Fama, Eugene F. 1972. "Components of Investment Performance." *Journal of Finance* 28 (3): 551–67.

This truly seminal paper was the first to suggest decomposing the returns of a portfolio in the manner the author proposes. Fama suggests finer breakdowns of performance than given by the Sharpe, Treynor, or Jensen. For example, methods are presented for distinguishing, on the one hand, the part of an observed return that results from ability to pick the best securities of a given level of risk ("selectivity") from, on the other hand, the part that is a result of predictions of general market price movements ("timing"). The author also suggests methods for measuring the effects of forgone diversification when an investment manager decides to concentrate the portfolio's holdings in what the manager thinks are a few "winners."

Fama, Eugene F., and Kenneth R. French. 1993. "Common Risk Factors in Stock and Bond Returns." *Journal of Financial Economics* 33: 3–56.

The authors propose that three common factors can empirically explain the cross-relationships between stock returns: an overall market factor and factors related to size and value. This paper sets forth the widely used Fama–French three-factor model.

Fama, Eugene F., and Kenneth R. French. 2015. "A Five-Factor Asset Pricing Model." *Journal of Financial Economics* 116 (1): 1–22.

The authors propose that a five-factor model is better than the three-factor model.

Feibel, B.J. 2003. *Investment Performance Measurement*. John Wiley & Sons.

This wide-ranging book on investment performance measurement is valuable for its in-depth spreadsheet examples of attribution analysis. Part IV of five parts describes performance attribution.

Fischer, Bernd, and Russell Wermers. 2013. *Performance Evaluation and Attribution of Security Portfolios*. Elsevier.

A substantial work on performance evaluation, this book includes detailed chapters on equity attribution, fixed-income attribution, analysis of multi-asset-class portfolios and hedge funds, and attribution analysis with derivatives.

Fisher, Jeffery D., and Joseph D'Alessandro. 2019. "Risk-Adjusted Performance Analysis of Real Estate Portfolios." Working paper. https://www.ncreif.org/globalassets/public-site/research/ncreif-insights/risk-adjusted-attribution-analysis-of-real-estate-portfolios-7-28-19-final---copy-for-ncreif-website.pdf.

This article proposes a risk-adjusted performance attribution analysis that integrates risk measures with the Brinson models of attribution. The benefit is that it allows analysts to decompose the excess portfolio return into components of risk allocation, selection, and net selectivity that are additive and consistent with financial theory.

Frongello, Andrew S.B. 2002a. "Attribution Linking: Proofed and Clarified." *Journal of Performance Measurement* 7 (1): 54–67.

The author provides the mathematical proofs for attribution linking while illustrating the importance of order dependence. He also critiques the multiperiod Brinson methodology suggested by Laker (2002).

Frongello, Andrew S.B. 2002b. "Linking Single Period Attribution Results." *Journal of Performance Measurement* 6 (3): 10–22.

This article proposes a linking algorithm that allows the summing of single-period attribution to arrive at cumulative results that explain the exact difference in cumulative returns. In addition to the judgement criteria introduced by Carino (1999), the author adds the criteria of sincerity, intuitive, and order dependence.

Frongello, Andrew S.B. 2006. "Linking of Attribution Results." In *Portfolio Analysis*, edited by Timothy P. Ryan, 343–68. Risk Books.

The author reviews popular linking methodologies and provides descriptions and examples of small differences. His conclusion is that although the mathematics may differ greatly from one method to another, the story told by the resulting attribution is the same regardless of the method.

Giguere, Claude. 2003. "Transaction-Based vs Holdings-Based Attribution: A Perspective." *Journal of Performance Measurement* 8 (1): 24–26.

The author defines transaction-based and holdings-based attribution and expresses a strong preference for the transaction-based approach.

Giguere, Claude. 2005. "Thinking through Fixed Income Attribution—Reflections from a Group of French Practitioners." *Journal of Performance Measurement* 9 (4): 46–65.

The author provides reflections on a group of practitioners whose objectives were to review the theoretical and methodological aspects of fixed-income attribution and to define best practices. In the context of fixed income, this group agreed to the following:

- Excess return is generally low; therefore, methodologies must be accurate with small residuals.
- The attribution results must match the investment decision process.
- The price differential between the portfolio and the benchmark is not an effect attributable to the manager.
- The calculation frequency should be as high as possible to avoid distortion.

The group described two types of attribution:

1. Yield-curve decomposition, which breaks down performance into passage of time, yield-curve movements (however described), and spread variations. This analysis is mostly intended for portfolio managers.

2. Exposure decomposition, a top-down approach based on intermediate reference portfolios. It can be better understood by noninvestment professionals than yield-curve decomposition and is useful when explaining the source of added value.

Gillet, Philippe, and Bernard Hommolie. 2006. "Fixed Income Attribution: A Combined Methodology." *Journal of Performance Measurement* 10 (4): 64–78.

The authors describe two existing forms of fixed-income performance attribution—"successive portfolios" and "successive spreads"—and suggest a combined model.

GRAP. 1997. "Synthèse des modèles d'attribution de performance." Paris: Groupe de Recherche en Attribution de Performance (March).

This early publication of a multiperiod arithmetic linking algorithm was created by a French working group of performance measurement experts.

Grinold, Richard C., and Ronald N. Kahn. 1995. *Active Portfolio Management.* Irwin Professional Publishing.

This encyclopaedic work on quantitative equity investing sets forth, among many other concepts, the "Fundamental Law of Active Management" the observation that the information ratio of any trading strategy is proportional to the square root of the number of independent bets made per year.

Heatter, Craig, Charles Gabriel, and Yi Wang. 2004. "A Four-Factor Performance Attribution Model for Equity Portfolios." *Journal of Performance Measurement* 9 (1): 51–59.

The authors discuss Carhart's (1997) four-factor model in the context of performance attribution. They are able to identify and accurately quantify a portfolio's risk exposures, sources of excess return, and sources of added value.

Hensel, Chris R., D. Don Ezra, and John H. Ilkiw. 1991. "The Importance of the Asset Allocation Decision." *Financial Analysts Journal* 47 (4): 65–72.

Building on the work of Brinson, Hood, and Beebower (1986), the authors suggest that if US T-bills are the appropriate naive alternative for US investors, then asset allocation away from T-bills is, as commonly thought, the single decision with the greatest impact on an investor's return. But if a diversified mix is the alternative, then the impact of departing from this alternative may be no greater than the impact of other decisions, including security selection.

Holbrook, J.P. 1977. "Investment Performance of Pension Funds." *Journal of the Institute of Actuaries* 104 (1): 15–91.

This important paper pulls together the work of the BAI (1968), Fama (1972), and the Society of Investment Analysts (SIA 1972). The article establishes the importance of investment objectives, the nature of liabilities, the need for investment policies, and the responsibilities of trustees. Crucially, the author decomposes the decision-making process into policy decisions, strategy decisions, and selection. Holbrook suggests the use of notional funds for each step of the decision process and establishes a geometric relationship for the value added (or subtracted) at each step of the process.

Hsu, Jason C., Vitali Kalesnik, and Brett W. Myers. 2010. "Performance Attribution: Measuring Dynamic Allocation Skill." *Financial Analysts Journal* 66 (6): 17–26.

The authors propose an extension of the Brinson model that subdivides asset allocation into static and dynamic components.

Hymans, Clifford, and John Mulligan. 1980. *The Measurement of Portfolio Performance*. Kluwer Publishing.

This extremely useful early book on performance measurement includes, in particular, a useful history of the subject to 1980, together with appropriate references. Chapter 18 on performance analysis brings Holbrook's work to a wider audience beyond UK actuaries, and Appendix 6 provides a worked example of attribution.

Ibbotson, Roger G., and Rex A. Sinquefield. 1982. *Stocks, Bonds, Bills, and Inflation: The Past and the Future*. Charlottesville, VA: CFA Institute Research Foundation.

The authors document, from a starting date of 1926, the monthly and annual returns on US stocks, bonds, T-bills, and what they call "inflation" (a hypothetical asset returning the rate of change in the US CPI). They calculate historical (achieved) risk premiums based on differences between the average returns of these assets and make probabilistic projections of future returns.

Illmer, Stefan J. 2009. "Decomposing the Money-Weighted Rate of Return—an Update." *Journal of Performance Measurement* 14 (1): 22–29.

This paper illustrates two methodologies that help analysts understand where historical return (expressed as an internal rate of return) and historical profit and loss are coming from. The author suggests that money-weighted attribution has a lot of advantages because its results are in line with profit-and-loss attribution and it correctly separates the timing effect between the asset allocation and stock-picking effects.

Illmer, Stefan J., and Wolfgang Marty. 2003. "Decomposing the Money-Weighted Rate of Return." *Journal of Performance Measurement* 7 (4): 42–50.

This article addresses return attribution from a client's point of view. It illustrates the decomposition of the money-weighted rate of return and shows its relationship to the time-weighted rate of return.

Jiang, Yindeng, and Joseph Saenz. 2014/2015. "The Associative Property of Attribution Linking." *Journal of Performance Measurement* 19 (2): 19–24.

The authors suggest that the "associative" property is necessary for attribution linking. Among the popular smoothing/linking methods, they show that Carino (1999) and Frongello (2002a) are associative, whereas Menchero (2000) and various *ad hoc* methods are not. They also suggest that Frongello and Carino produce similar results.

Karnosky, Denis S., and Brian D. Singer. 1994. *Global Asset Management and Performance Attribution*. Charlottesville, VA: Research Foundation of the Institute of Chartered Financial Analysts.

The most important work written on performance attribution in the 1990s, this book develops an analytical framework for evaluating global asset markets and uses that framework to construct a performance attribution system that isolates the effects of market allocation, currency management, and security selection on global portfolios.

This book is important for demonstrating that a multinational portfolio is suboptimally managed if currency is not managed independently and for demonstrating the importance of interest rate differentials between currencies.

Kingston, T.D. 1973. "Measuring Investment Performance [with discussion]." In *Transactions of the Faculty of Actuaries* 34: 241–98. Cambridge University Press.

This work is another early paper on the whole subject of measuring investment performance. Section 3 deals particularly with performance attribution. Methods are suggested for comparing actual rates of return with those of indexes, notional portfolios, and other funds. Of most interest is the formal record of the discussion after the paper's presentation. Note the response from Mr Stewart (pp. 268–74), which documents the now familiar Brinson and Fachler (1985) method (Method 2) and Brinson et al. (1986)

method (Method 1) formulas at least 10 years before the Brinson papers were published.

Kirievsky, Leonid, and Anatoly Kirievsky. 2000. "Attribution Analysis: Combining Attribution Effects over Time Made Easy." *Journal of Performance Measurement* 4 (4): 49–59.

The authors propose a smoothing algorithm that consists of "separating pure effects from changes in each factor and the remainder (cross-product)".

Kirievsky, Leonid, and Anatoly Kirievsky. 2004. "Attribution Analysis: Old and New." *Journal of Performance Measurement* 9 (1): 60–74.

In this article, the authors describe in detail the problem of attribution analysis and provide a precise method of solving it. They analyse the shortcomings of other multiperiod linking and smoothing algorithms and the geometric model and critique the original Brinson et al. (1986) paper. Based on an example of historical Australian funds data, they suggest that security selection is the main determinant of return.

Kophamel, Andrew. 2003. "Risk-Adjusted Performance Attribution: A New Paradigm for Performance Analysis." *Journal of Performance Measurement* 7 (4): 51–62.

This article proposes a three-dimensional approach to link risk and return via the intuitive construct of volume and the "performance cube" rather than using the familiar two-dimensional areas of the Brinson model.

Laker, Damian. 2000. "What Is This Thing Called 'Interaction'?" *Journal of Performance Measurement* 5 (1): 43–57.

In this paper, the author suggests that the interaction term has a bad reputation. He states that portfolio managers do not distinguish between interaction and error terms but arbitrarily add them to other terms. As a result, they find interaction difficult to explain to clients.

The author argues that the interaction term is sometimes more explanatory than the other attributes and that attempts to avoid confusion by "getting rid of" the interaction term in a Brinson model are, in fact, likely to create more confusion.

Laker, Damian. 2001. "Incorporating Transaction Cost Measurement into Performance Attribution." *Journal of Performance Measurement* 5 (4): 13–24.

This paper points out that transaction costs (explicit costs, such as brokerage and taxes, and implicit costs, such as the bid–offer spread, market impact, and opportunity cost) are not dealt with explicitly in most performance attribution methods and are normally included in the stock selection effect. The author suggests a stock-level, bottom-up style of attribution approach that identifies and separates the impact of intraday timing and transaction costs.

Laker, Damian. 2002. "A View from Down-Under." *Journal of Performance Measurement* 6 (4): 5–13.

The author suggests an exact method for multiperiod arithmetic attribution at a total level that can be used to evaluate the accuracy of various linking and smoothing methods, including naive compounding.

Laker, Damian. 2003. "Perspectives on Transaction-Based Attribution." *Journal of Performance Measurement* 8 (1): 10–23.

The author defines transaction-based attribution, holdings-based attribution, and transaction-based attribution that identifies transaction costs, and he provides worked examples of each. The paper explains that the simplicity, reduced number of calculations, and reduced data burden of holdings-based attribution come at the cost of accuracy.

Laker, Damian. 2005. "Toward Consensus on Multiple-Period Arithmetic Attribution." *Journal of Performance Measurement* 9 (3): 26–37.

The author defends criticism of his "exact" method for calculating multiperiod attributes at the total-fund level.

Lord, Timothy J. 1997. "The Attribution of Portfolio and Index Returns in Fixed Income." *Journal of Performance Measurement* 2 (1): 45–57.

This paper focuses on performance attribution as it applies to fixed-income portfolios and indexes. More clearly described as bottom-up contribution analysis of the portfolio compared with its benchmark, this paper emphasizes the requirement for the attribution to be consistent with the investment strategy of the portfolio manager. Income and price returns are calculated separately. Price return is then attributed according to duration, yield-curve distribution, sector allocation, and issue selection. Shift and twist are considered components of duration return; and sector and specific issuer effects are considered components of spread return. Included also are a calendar return (the price return resulting solely from the passage of time) and a residual return (the difference between the actual return and the model's estimate of return).

McLaren, Andrew. 2001. "A Geometric Methodology for Performance Attribution." *Journal of Performance Measurement* 5 (4): 45–57.

The author proposes a framework for absolute and relative multicurrency geometric attribution.

McLaren, Andrew. 2002. "A Framework for Multiple Currency Fixed Income Attribution." *Journal of Performance Measurement* 6 (4): 59–79.

This article presents a framework for analysing the investment decisions of a multicurrency fixed-income portfolio. The significant difference from the classical model is the addition of a reference yield-curve portfolio to measure the return generated from interest rate exposure decisions.

Menchero, Jose G. 2000. "An Optimized Approach to Linking Attribution Effects over Time." *Journal of Performance Measurement* 5 (1): 36–42.

In this paper, the author presents an intuitive and robust algorithm for linking single-period attribution effects over time. The method consists of first deducing the correct scaling between the single-period excess returns and the linked excess return and then optimally distributing the residual among the different time periods.

Menchero, Jose G. 2000/2001. "A Fully Geometric Approach to Performance Attribution." *Journal of Performance Measurement* 5 (2): 22–30.

In this paper, the author examines the close relationship between geometric and arithmetic calculations and their effects and uses the analogy to arrive at an intuitive mathematical form for attribution analysis. Also, while addressing the issues involved in aggregating the attribution effects across sectors, the author shows how they can be linked across time.

Menchero, Jose G. 2002/2003. "Performance Attribution with Short Positions." *Journal of Performance Measurement* 7 (2): 39–50.

In this paper, the author shows how classical attribution analysis can be adapted to include short positions. The keys to the methodology are

- explicit inclusion of the cash positions and
- independent treatment of the long and short sides of each sector.

Menchero, Jose G. 2003. "Linking Differences Do Matter." *Journal of Performance Measurement* 7 (3): 47–50.

In this short article, the author refutes the claim that differences between smoothing and linking algorithms are immaterial.

Menchero, Jose G., and Ben Davis. 2009. "Multi-Currency Performance Attribution." *Journal of Performance Measurement* 14 (1): 45–55.

The authors present a comprehensive model for attributing the performance of multicurrency portfolios based on the Karnosky and Singer (1994) framework but with certain refinements. In particular, they explicitly account for the cross-product effect derived from repatriating local profits back to the base currency of the investor.

Menchero, Jose G., and Junmin Hu. 2003. "Errors in Transaction-Based Performance Attribution." *Journal of Performance Measurement* 8 (1): 57–69.

The authors identify three types of transaction-based attribution: true time-weighted methods that use a buy-and-hold assumption and two types of transaction-based attribution based on modified Dietz return calculations. The two latter types are as follows: Type 1, which accounts for external and internal cash flows, and Type 2, which accounts for internal cash flows only. The authors acknowledge that the holdings-based approach will lead to differences between the actual return and the computed return, but they suggest that the magnitude should be small and typically depend on volatility and portfolio turnover. They suggest that this difference should be attributed to trading effects. The authors show that both Type 1 and Type 2 approaches will lead to attribution errors, so they ultimately prefer the holdings-based approach.

Mirabelli, Andre. 2000/2001. "The Structure and Visualization of Performance Attribution." *Journal of Performance Measurement* 5 (2): 55–80.

This paper proposes an alternative to multiperiod arithmetic performance attribution methods.

Modigliani, Leah. 1997. "Risk-Adjusted Performance, Part 1: The Time for Risk Measurement Is Now." *Morgan Stanley's Investment Perspectives* (February).

The author introduces the risk-adjusted return measure M2. The measure was developed by Franco Modigliani and his granddaughter Leah Modigliani.

Murira, Bernard, and Hector Sierra. 2006. "Fixed Income Attribution: A Unified Framework—Part 1." *Journal of Performance Measurement* 11 (1): 23–35.

This article provides a framework for understanding fixed-income performance attribution. The article discusses two complementary types of attribution model: (1) a factor model that captures the impact on the portfolio return of changes in economic variables, such as the term structure of interest rates, volatility, and prepayment speed, and (2) an allocation model that assesses the returns in excess of the benchmark returns of the allocation strategy in various sectors.

Murira, Bernard, and Hector Sierra. 2006/2007. "Fixed Income Attribution: A Unified Framework—Part 2." *Journal of Performance Measurement* 11 (2): 8–21.

A continuation of Part 1 (Murira and Sierra 2006/2007), this part discusses some practical issues related to the attribution process—in particular, the fact that duration is not a perfect measure. Other issues addressed are key-rate duration versus partial duration, selecting the appropriate point to use on the yield curve, dealing with transactions, linking multiperiod returns, and the accuracy of security prices.

Obeid, Alexander. 2005. "Reformulating Ankrim's Risk-Adjusted Performance Attribution." *Journal of Performance Measurement* 9 (3): 8–25.

This paper builds on the work of Ankrim (1992) but presents a more adequate risk adjustment for evaluating market timing.

O'Shea, Luis, and Vishv Jeet. 2018. "Single-Period Brinson-Style Performance Attribution for Private Capital." Working paper, Burgiss Applied Research (June).

In this working paper, the authors develop a methodology for Brinson-style attribution of private capital returns.

Ramaswamy, Srichander. 2001. "Fixed Income Portfolio Management: Risk Modeling, Portfolio Construction and Performance Attribution." *Journal of Performance Measurement* 5 (4): 58–70.

The author outlines a methodology for risk modelling, portfolio construction, and performance attribution of fixed-income portfolios.

Reztsov, Andrei. 2011/2012. "Geometric and Arithmetic Approaches to Attribution Linking Are Equivalent." *Journal of Performance Measurement* 16 (2): 46–56.

The author offers an algorithm that is not order dependent and has a linear nonsmoothing construction.

Sharpe, William F. 1988. "Determining a Fund's Effective Asset Mix." *Investment Management Review* (December): 59–69.

This landmark paper was the first to present return-based style analysis (attribution identifying exposure to growth, value, large-cap, and small-cap factors as well as the market factor). Sharpe describes the returns as leaving "tracks in the sand" that can be interpreted, by using regression analysis, as style exposures.

Sharpe, William F. 1992. "Asset Allocation: Management Style and Performance Measurement." *Journal of Portfolio Management* 18 (2): 7–19.

The author, building on Sharpe (1988), suggests a 12-asset-class model that determines the passive return of a notional portfolio having the same style as the asset manager. The manager's selection return is the difference between the actual return and the passive return in the same style.

SIA. 1972. *The Measurement of Portfolio Performance for Pension Funds.* Society of Investment Analysts.

Toward the end of 1970, a working group was set up by the UK Society of Investment Analysts to make recommendations on the subject of portfolio performance measurement for pension funds. The resulting report specifically puts forward methods of calculating portfolio performance, thus making possible a general comparison of funds.

The approach recommended has two aims: (1) the calculation of a rate of return for comparing funds and (2) the decomposition of the performance of a fund into two components—selection of stocks and selection of sectors. This report is, therefore, really the starting point of performance attribution because it both defines stock selection and sector allocation (called "sector selection" in the report) and provides a worked example.

Silva, Antonio F.A., Pablo J.C. de Carvalho, and Jose R.H. Ornelas. 2010. "A Performance Attribution Methodology for Fixed Income Portfolios." Portfolio and Risk Management for Central Banks and Sovereign Wealth Funds (February).

This paper presents a simple fixed-income attribution model suitable for the investment process of central banks. The approach does not require a specific methodology for yield-curve fitting.

Simmons, Peter, and Anton Karadakov. 2013/2014. "A Simplified Fixed Income Performance Attribution Model." *Journal of Performance Measurement* 18 (2): 44–55.

The authors create an attribution model that follows a top-down approach but is built from the bottom up. The attribution groups the output into five sections: duration management, spread management, issue selection, yield management, and currency management.

Singer, Brian D. 1996. "Evaluation of Portfolio Performance: Attribution Analysis." *Journal of Performance Measurement* 1 (2): 45–55.

The author explains that attribution analysis is an important aid in the critical review of active strategies and in the decision-making process for a portfolio. This article provides a basic framework for gleaning accurate information regarding active portfolio management decisions.

Spaulding, David. 2002. "Is Linking Attribution Effects as Hard as It Looks?" *Journal of Performance Measurement* 6 (3): 32–39.

The author compares a number of smoothing and linking algorithms.

Spaulding, David. 2003a. "Holdings- vs. Transaction-Based Attribution: An Overview." *Journal of Performance Measurement* 8 (1): 52–56.

The author concludes that the question "which is better?" has no simple answer. Too many variables are at work. Some firms' trading volumes are such that a simple buy-and-hold model will not provide even the remotest degree of precision. But how much more must a firm spend? And for many firms, any incremental benefit can be justified by the added cost.

Spaulding, David. 2003b. *Investment Performance Attribution*. McGraw-Hill.

The book is the first devoted solely to the subject of performance attribution.

Spaulding, David. 2003/2004. "Demystifying the Interaction Effect." *Journal of Performance Measurement* 8 (2): 49–54.

The author explains that the interaction effect is the product of two decisions: selection and allocation. Despite pointing out potentially misleading results caused by calculating interaction (for example, mispriced securities and/or investing in sectors not in the benchmark), the author determines that on balance, it is better to calculate interaction, take the time to do some analysis, and then decide where to assign it—better yet would be to show the interaction as a separate item and prepare to explain it.

Spaulding, David. 2016. "Performance Attribution Risk-Adjusted: Why It Makes Sense and How to Do It." *Journal of Performance Measurement* 20 (4): 42–56.

This paper briefly reviews various risk-adjusted attribution methodologies and suggests a simple methodology based on M^2 (the Modigliani and Modigliani risk-adjusted performance measure).

Spaulding, David. 2018. "Transaction- vs. Holdings-Based Attribution: The Differences Are Not So Clear but Quite Important." *Journal of Performance Measurement* 22 (3): 49–76.

In this detailed study, the author finds that the residuals caused by holdings-based analysis can be extensive and are not necessarily correlated with turnover, as might be expected.

Spaulding, David, and Stephen Campisi. 2007. "A Case for Money-Weighted Attribution." *Journal of Performance Measurement* 11 (Performance Attribution Supplement: 8–20.

The authors make the case for money-weighted attribution. Since cash flow movements are a factor that defines the investment process, cash flows must be part of the performance measurement and evaluation process and should not be neutralised, as they are in a time-weighted calculation. The authors point out that transaction-based attribution methodologies that use modified Dietz calculations are, in fact, money-weighted attributions over a single period.

Stannard, John C. 1997. "Measuring Investment Returns of Portfolios Containing Derivatives: Part II—Performance Attribution." *Journal of Performance Measurement* 1 (3): 5–9.

This paper demonstrates that a derivatives position can be represented as a series of (normally, two or more) notional asset exposures representing physical securities and any implied borrowing used to finance the security position. Standard performance attribution techniques can be used on notional assets to represent the derivatives in terms of the underlying investment decisions.

Surz, Ronald J. 1999/2000. "Attribution with Style." *Journal of Performance Measurement* 4 (2): 50–64.

This paper makes the case that manager style is a powerful determinant of performance. Style-based attribution produces much more reliable indicators than sector-based methods because most investment managers manage to a style rather than to some mix of economic sectors. Using sector-based attribution analysis can produce significantly misleading inferences.

Van Breukelen, Gerard. 2000. "Fixed Income Attribution." *Journal of Performance Measurement* 4 (4): 61–68.

This article discusses performance attribution for fixed-income portfolios. The starting point is a top-down decision structure, which means that the portfolio's overall duration is decided first, followed by the distribution over markets. The risk factor for markets is a combination of weight and duration. After the market allocation, individual issue selection is measured. Currency allocation is independent and measured separately.

Wagner, Wayne H., and Dennis A. Tito. 1977. "Definitive New Measures of Bond Performance and Risk." *Pension World* (May): 17–26.

This article is an early attempt to analyse fixed-income portfolios in a manner similar to Fama (1972) decomposition but replacing beta with duration.

Weber, Arno. 2018. "Geometric Attribution and the Interaction Effect." *Journal of Performance Measurement* 22 (4): 6–19.

The author presents a variant of the Burnie, Knowles, and Teder (1998) model that includes interaction effects.

Wong, Celia. 2003/2004. "Attribution—Arithmetic or Geometric? The Best of Both Worlds." *Journal of Performance Measurement* 8 (2): 10–18.

The author lists the pros and cons of the arithmetic and geometric methods and concludes the geometric method is clearly superior in almost every way. The author states that the arithmetic method produces a distortion when applied to multiple-period attribution because returns naturally compound geometrically, not arithmetically. Nothing can be done to improve the arithmetic method to overcome this basic fact. What is not so well known is that the arithmetic method produces a distortion even for a single period when multiple currencies are involved. In conclusion, the author suggests a method that is computed geometrically and presented arithmetically.

Wong, Celia. 2007. "Comparing Arithmetic and Geometric Attribution." In *Advanced Portfolio Attribution Analysis*, edited by Carl Bacon, 135–59. Risk Books.

The author provides a new arithmetic formula that eliminates the drawbacks of multiperiod arithmetic attribution with no need for linking algorithms. She also presents an easy way of converting between arithmetic and geometric attribution so that expressing attribution results is just a matter of preference.

Zangari, Peter J., and Mehmet Bayraktar. 2005/2006. "Which Is Better: Daily or Monthly Attribution?" *Journal of Performance Measurement* 10 (2): 8–19.

This article explores important issues in the debate about the merits of daily versus monthly attribution and concludes that daily attribution, if done methodically, should produce results that are superior to monthly attribution.

Named Endowments

The CFA Institute Research Foundation acknowledges with sincere gratitude the generous contributions of the Named Endowment participants listed below.

Gifts of at least US$100,000 qualify donors for membership in the Named Endowment category, which recognizes in perpetuity the commitment toward unbiased, practitioner-oriented, relevant research that these firms and individuals have expressed through their generous support of the CFA Institute Research Foundation.

Ameritech
Anonymous
Robert D. Arnott
Theodore R. Aronson, CFA
Asahi Mutual Life Insurance Company
Batterymarch Financial Management
Boston Company
Boston Partners Asset Management, L.P.
Gary P. Brinson, CFA
Brinson Partners, Inc.
Capital Group International, Inc.
Concord Capital Management
Dai-Ichi Life Insurance Company
Daiwa Securities
Mr. and Mrs. Jeffrey Diermeier
Gifford Fong Associates
Investment Counsel Association of America, Inc.
Jacobs Levy Equity Management
John A. Gunn, CFA
John B. Neff, CFA
Jon L. Hagler Foundation
Long-Term Credit Bank of Japan, Ltd.
Lynch, Jones & Ryan, LLC
Meiji Mutual Life Insurance Company
Miller Anderson & Sherrerd, LLP
Nikko Securities Co., Ltd.
Nippon Life Insurance Company of Japan
Nomura Securities Co., Ltd.
Payden & Rygel
Provident National Bank
Frank K. Reilly, CFA
Salomon Brothers
Sassoon Holdings Pte. Ltd.
Scudder Stevens & Clark
Security Analysts Association of Japan
Shaw Data Securities, Inc.
Sit Investment Associates, Inc.
Standish, Ayer & Wood, Inc.
State Farm Insurance Company
Sumitomo Life America, Inc.
T. Rowe Price Associates, Inc.
Templeton Investment Counsel Inc.
Frank Trainer, CFA
Travelers Insurance Co.
USF&G Companies
Yamaichi Securities Co., Ltd.

Senior Research Fellows

Financial Services Analyst Association

For more on upcoming Research Foundation publications and webcasts, please visit www.cfainstitute.org/en/research/foundation.

Made in the USA
Las Vegas, NV
07 November 2026

57650027R00040